IDEALS AND REALITIES OF ISLAM

Seyyed Hossein Nasr was born in Tehran where he received his early education. He later studied in the West and received his B.S. from the Massachusetts Institute of Technology and his M.A. and Ph.D. from Harvard University, where he studied the History of Science and Learning with special concentration on Islamic science and philosophy. In 1958 he returned to Iran and taught at Tehran University where he was Professor of the History of Science and Philosophy. From 1974 he was also president and founder of the Iranian Academy of Philosophy. He is now Professor of Islamic Studies at the George Washington University, Washington DC, in the USA.

Other works by Seyyed Hossein Nasr in English

THREE MUSLIM SAGES
AN INTRODUCTION TO ISLAMIC COSMOLOGICAL DOCTRINES
SCIENCE AND CIVILIZATION IN ISLAM
AN ANNOTATED BIBLIOGRAPHY OF ISLAMIC SCIENCE
MAN AND NATURE: THE SPIRITUAL CRISIS OF MODERN MAN
ISLAM AND THE PLIGHT OF MODERN MAN
ISLAMIC SCIENCE: AN ILLUSTRATED STUDY
THE TRANSCENDENT THEOSOPHY OF SADR AL-DIN SHIRAZI
ISLAMIC LIFE AND THOUGHT
KNOWLEDGE AND THE SACRED
ISLAMIC ART AND SPIRITUALITY
TRADITIONAL ISLAM IN THE MODERN WORLD
THE NEED FOR A SACRED SCIENCE
THE ISLAMIC PHILOSOPHY OF SCIENCE
THE ESSENTIAL WRITINGS OF FRITHJOF SCHUON (ed.)
SHI'ISM (ed.)
EXPECTATION OF THE MILLENIUM (ed.)
ISLAMIC SPIRITUALITY I AND II (ed.)

Ideals and Realities of Islam

SEYYED HOSSEIN NASR

Mandala
An Imprint of HarperCollins*Publishers*

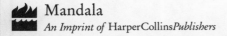

Mandala
An Imprint of HarperCollins*Publishers*
77–85 Fulham Palace Road,
Hammersmith, London W6 8JB

First published in Great Britain by George Allen & Unwin 1966
First published in Unwin Paperbacks (Mandala) 1979
This impression published by Mandala 1991
10 9 8 7 6 5 4 3

A CIP catalogue record for this book
is available from the British Library

ISBN 0 04 297049 0

Printed in Great Britain by Mackays of Chatham, Kent

In the Name of Allah Most Merciful and Compassionate

The essays comprising this book grew out of a series of public lectures delivered at the American University of Beirut during the academic year 1964–65. During this time the Aga Khan Chair of Islamic studies was established at the University and I was invited to become its first occupant. Situated at Beirut, at the meeting place between East and West, between the Islamic world and the Occident, in a land where different branches of Islam are well represented, the new Chair is meant to occupy a vital position in the world of Islamic studies, according to the wish of its donor. And it is in complying with his wish that this book is launched as the first written contribution from this Chair of Islamic studies to the world outside.

To fulfil the wish of His Highness the Aga Khan to convey the Chair's significance beyond the walls of the classrooms of the American University of Beirut, I undertook a series of fifteen public lectures entitled 'Dimensions of Islam' in which both the religion of Islam and diverse aspects of the civilization created by this tradition were discussed. This volume contains the first six lectures dealing with Islam itself. It is hoped to publish the second part of the series dealing with the spiritual, intellectual and artistic life of Islam and the interaction of Islam with other civilizations in a separate volume. I have been encouraged in undertaking this task by the enthusiasm of a large and receptive audience and the request of many people near and far to have the lectures in printed form.

It is my belief that the duty of the Aga Khan Chair is to endeavour to present Islam and its intellectual treasures in a contemporary language, faithfully, and without deviating from the traditional point of view. It should also undertake the task of carrying out a dialogue with other religions, particularly Christianity, which meets Islam in Lebanon. And it should seek to study the different schools within Islam which are again well represented in the country where the Chair is located.

This situation of the Chair in a Western-oriented university in the East also places a particular responsibility upon it. It is urgent for the Islamic world today to come to know modernism in its true nature and to give the Islamic answer to so many pseudo-intellectual fads that parade as the truth and allure the younger generation away from the eternal truths contained within Islam. The Chair is eminently suited to undertake this challenge. It could be instrumental in the task that the Islamic world faces to answer the claims of such modern ideas as materialism, evolution, scientism, existentialism, historicism, etc. In this way it could also aid in providing an Islamic answer to the studies of the orientalists—many of which are in fact based on such modern notions.

In many parts of the Islamic world, particularly in those countries where modern education is more prevalent, the younger generation has no knowledge of the intellectual and spiritual aspects of Islam, and is completely defenceless before the onslaught of modernism. That is why with the first contact with Western science, philosophy or literature so many young Muslims lose their spiritual balance and feel estranged from their own tradition. Everywhere there is a profound need for presenting the verities of Islam, especially in their intellectual and spiritual aspect, in a language which those brought up in the modern educational system can comprehend.

There are very few works in European languages which treat Islam from its own point of view, from within the tradition. And as far as the languages of the Islamic people are concerned many good works exist in them which are, however, couched in arguments addressed to the traditional Muslim intelligentsia in whose mind there are not the same doubts and difficulties that face the modernized segment of society. The arguments of the traditional religious authorities are completely valid and their language is all that it should be. It is not they who should be criticized. Rather, the anomalous situation of the times has brought about a condition in which the language and line of argument has to be modified to appeal to and be understood by the Western educated Muslims or those who are affected by the modern mentality.

It is our hope that the Chair can become instrumental in the realization of all these goals which are vital to the Islamic world and towards whose solution all Muslims should endeavour. And it is as a very humble contribution towards the achievement of some of these ends that this volume is presented.

The book seeks most of all to outline the essential aspects of Islam as an ever-living force, and not just as a matter of historical interest, in a language that is contemporary and in fact is addressed to those who are acquainted with the dialectic of modern thought. Moreover, I have tried to answer in many cases the charges made by Western works against Islam especially as it concerns such fundamental elements of the faith as the Quran and the *Hadîth*. The whole line of argument is therefore coloured by what has been written already on Islam in European languages so that some of the discussions may even appear redundant to someone not acquainted with such writings. I have not sought to criticize orientalism purely and simply but to present the point of view of Islam and show why in several instances the view of certain Western scholars cannot be accepted by Muslims.

Also in these essays I have attempted to present what is most universal in Islam and underlies the beliefs of all the orthodox branches of the tradition. Throughout the book, especially when treating the very difficult and delicate problem of the relation between Sunnism and Shi'ism, it has not been my aim to gloss over sentimentally the existing differences, because these differences of perspective have been providentially placed within Islam. Rather, my task has been to show that these two major groups in Islam are unified in the essential principles, and that each presents an interpretation of the faith which is complete in itself. Likewise, it has been my aim to discuss the central role of Sufism and its unifying function in Islam in both the intellectual and social domains.

Finally, without devoting a particular essay to the study of other religions, I have made references to other great traditions trying to show the profound similarities which exist between all religions. At the same time I have avoided the prevalent view of considering all religions to be exactly the same, by pointing to both the similarities and the differences of structure between Islam and other religions, and especially Christianity to which more reference has been made considering the audience to which these lectures were addressed. Moreover, although a separate study has not been devoted to the discussion of different modern ideas, the Islamic response to many modern challenges has been stated either directly or by allusion.

The question treated in each essay is the subject of not only one but of many books so that it has not been possible to be exhaustive. I have in fact sought in each essay to remain faithful as far as possible to the original lecture so that the length of each chapter is determined by the lecture's limited duration. It has been my aim in treating each subject to concern myself with the principles involved and not the detailed history which can be found in many other sources.

In drawing the material for these essays I have relied first and foremost on Islamic sources, on the Quran, the *Ḥâdith* and traditional authorities. It is in fact the traditional Muslim view that I have sought to present here. But also, I have drawn from those works of orientalists which are of value from a scientific and historical point of view, especially the writings of Sir Hamilton Gibb, Louis Massignon and Henry Corbin. As far as sources in European languages are concerned I have also relied substantially for both the means of presentation and the method of approach on the works of contemporary traditional authors in the West such as Titus Burckhardt, Marco Pallis, Martin Lings, René Guénon, and especially Frithjof Schuon whose *Understanding Islam* has been a constant source of guidance for me. I believe this work to be the most outstanding ever written in a European language on why Muslims believe in Islam and why Islam offers to man all that he needs religiously and spiritually.

In order to enable readers of this work to carry out their studies further I have given a selected annotated bibliography at the end of each chapter. The list of works cited has been drawn most of all from writings of Muslim authors and also of those orientalists who are sympathetic towards Islam or whose works are of special scientific value. In no case has the bibliography meant to be exhaustive and its scope has been limited to works in European languages, especially in English and French.

In conclusion I wish to thank His Highness the Aga Khan for having made it possible for me to deliver the lectures which form the basis of this work. I am also grateful to the Faculty of Arts and Sciences and especially the Department of History of the American University of Beirut for having sponsored these public lectures, and to Professor Yusuf Ibish and Mr. Kamal Khan for the innumerable ways in which they have facilitated my activities as the first occupant of the Aga Khan Chair and have aided in the realization of this volume.

Introduction

It is hoped that this collection of essays and the public lectures upon which they are based will serve as a humble foundation for the activities of the Aga Khan Chair of Islamic Studies at the American University of Beirut. May the Chair be honoured to become one of the most important of its kind. May it realize its full possibilities with the Will of Allah.

Beirut
Ramadan 1384
January 1965

CONTENTS

CHAPTER I

Islam, the Last Religion and the Primordial Religion—Its Universal and Particular Traits

Every revealed religion is *the* religion and *a* religion, *the* religion in as much as it contains within itself the Truth and means of attaining the Truth, *a* religion since it emphasizes a particular aspect of the Truth in conformity with the spiritual and psychological needs of the humanity for whom it is destined and to whom it is addressed. Religion itself is derived from the word *religio* which means to bind. It is that which binds man to the truth. As such every religion possesses ultimately two essential elements which are its basis and foundation: a doctrine which distinguishes between the Absolute and the relative, between the absolutely Real and the relatively real, between that which has absolute value and that whose value is relative; and a method of concentrating upon the Real, of attaching oneself to the Absolute and living according to the Will of Heaven in accordance with the purpose and meaning of human existence.

These two elements, the doctrine and the method, the means of distinguishing between what is Real and what appears to be real, and attaching oneself to the Real, exist in every orthodox and integral religion and are in fact the essence of every religion. No religion, whether it be Islam or Christianity, Hinduism or Buddhism, can be without a doctrine as to what is Absolute and what is relative. Only the doctrinal language differs from one tradition to another. Nor can any religion be without a method of concentrating on the Real and living according to It although the means again differ in different traditional climates.

Every religion believes in a transcendent Reality that stands above the world of change and becoming. Yet, no religion has claimed that the world on its own level of existence is completely unreal. Even the Hindu *māyā* is not so much illusion as the 'Divine play' or *līla* which veils and hides the Absolute. Were the world and the soul to be completely unreal there would be no meaning in trying to attach the soul to the Real, to the Absolute. The doctrine is thus a discrimination between the Absolute and the relative, between grades of reality, degrees of universal existence. And the method is precisely the means of attaching the relatively real to the absolutely Real once one realizes that the reality of the soul and the world that surrounds it is not absolute but relative, that both the soul and the world derive their sustenance from a Reality that transcends both the soul *and* the world.

Now, Islam like every orthodox religion is comprised of a doctrine and a method and it is for us to see how the Islamic revelation deals with these cardinal elements, how it envisages the relation between man and God. It is of course God who is the Absolute and man the relative. And it is for man to come to realize this truth, to know that only God is God, that is, only He is the Absolute, and that man is a relative being who stands before Him given the free choice of either accepting or rejecting His Will.

This relation between man and God, or the relative and the Absolute is central in every religion. Only each religion emphasizes a certain aspect of this relationship, while inwardly it contains the Truth as such in its teachings whatever the outward limitations of its forms might be. That is why to have lived any religion fully is to have lived all religions and there is nothing more meaningless and even pernicious than to create a syncretism from various religions with a claim to universality while in reality one is doing nothing less than destroying the revealed forms which alone make the attachment of the relative to the Absolute, of man to God, possible. Without the 'dictum of heaven', without revelation in its universal sense, no religion is possible and man cannot attach himself to God without God having himself through His grace provided the means for man to do so. Every orthodox religion is the choice of heaven and while still intact contains both the doctrine and the method which 'save' man from his wretched terrestrial condition and open to him the gates of heaven.

In the confrontation of man and God, Islam does not emphasize the descent or incarnation or manifestation of the Absolute, nor the fallen, imperfect and sinful nature of man. Rather, it considers man as he is in his essential nature and God as He is in his absolute Reality. The Islamic perspective is based upon the consideration of the Divine Being as He is in Himself not as He is incarnated in history. It is based on the Absolute and not on the 'descent of the Absolute'. Likewise, Islam considers man not as what he has become after that very significant event which Christianity calls original sin and 'fall' but as man is in his primordial nature, in his *fiṭrah*, a nature which he bears deep down within his soul.

It might of course be said that not only Islam but every religion is based on God and man's relation to Him. But there are certain religions which emphasize a particular incarnation of the Divinity or various manifestations of the Absolute. In the non-theistic climate of Buddhism emphasis is laid on the 'Void' and the Buddha himself who is the 'manifestation of the Void' (or *shunya*); and in Christianity it is the personality of Christ that is particularly emphasized and is central so that quite naturally the religion that Christ founded is called Christianity. But the case of Islam is quite different and for this very reason it is fallacious to call Islam Mohammadanism, although this term has been used so long in Western languages that it is difficult to eradicate its use completely.

Islam is a religion based not on the personality of the founder but on Allah Himself. The Prophet is the channel through whom man received a message pertaining to the nature of the Absolute and subsequently the relative, a message which contains a doctrine and a method. Therefore, it is Allah Himself who is the central reality of the religion, and the role of the Prophet in Islam and Christ in Christianity are thereby quite different at the same time that naturally as 'messengers of God' they also bear similarities to each other. Islam emphasizes over and over again not how God has manifested Himself but what His nature is—nature in the common meaning of the word not in the philosophical sense, for philosophically speaking Allah has no nature. It would, therefore be more in conformity with the

Islamic perspective to call it 'Allahism' if need be rather than the prevalent Mohammadanism.

As for man, Islam legislates for him according to his real nature as he is with all the possibilities inherent in the human state as such. But what does 'man as he is' mean? Seen in his ordinary condition man is a weak and negligent being. He is usually subservient to his surroundings and a prisoner of his own lust and animal passions. He does not know what it really means to be man and does not live to the full potentialities of his human condition. Were it to be otherwise he would need no religion and revelation to guide him. Islam without in any way overlooking the limited and weak aspect of human nature does not consider man in his aspect as a perverted will but essentially as a theomorphic being who as the vicegerent (*khalīfah*) of God on earth is the central theophany (*tajallī*) of God's Names and Qualities.

There is something God-like in man as attested to by the Quranic statement, (Pickthall translation): 'I have made him and have breathed into him my spirit' (Quran XV, 29) (فاذا سويته ونفخت فيه من روحى) and by the tradition 'God created Adam upon His own form' (خلق الله آدم على صورته). God created Adam, the prototype of man, upon 'His own form', i.e., as a mirror reflecting in a central and conscious manner His Names and Qualities. There is therefore, something of a 'divine nature' (*malakūtī*) in man; and it is in the light of this profound nature in man that Islam envisages him.

This belief is not, however in any way anthropomorphic, for the Divine Essence (*al-dhāt*) remains absolutely transcendent and no religion has emphasized the transcendent aspect of God more than Islam. The Islamic concept of man as a theomorphic being is not an anthropomorphism. It does not make God into man. Rather, the Islamic revelation conceives of man as this theomorphic being and addresses itself to that something in man which is in the form of the 'Divine'. That something is first of all an intelligence that can discern between the true and the false or the real and the illusory and is naturally led to Unity or *tawḥīd*. Secondly, it is a will to choose freely between the true and the false, and thirdly it is the power of speech, of the word to be able to express the relationship between the Divinity and man. In Islam man is not first of all a perverted will who also possesses intelligence but an intelligence, which leads 'naturally' to the assertion of the Divine, who also possesses will and speech.

Now, intelligence, will and speech are all essentially Divine Qualities. It is God who has as one of His Qualities knowledge which is connected to the Divine Intellect. The Name *al-'alīm*, (العلم) he who knows, is one of the Divine Names, and it is also God who possesses absolute freedom. Being infinite there is nothing outside of Him to act as an obstacle to His freedom. God is the Infinite and only the Infinite is absolutely free. Also the Word belongs to God. It comes from Him, belongs to Him and returns to Him. The qualities of intelligence, will and speech are thus Divine Qualities which God has given in trust to man, and through them leads man back to Himself.

Islam takes these three elements, namely intelligence, will and speech, which one might say man has 'borrowed' from God, and makes them the basis of the religion, carrying these elements to the most profound and universal level of their meaning. Islam asks what is intelligence and what is its real nature. The real nature of intelligence is ultimately to come to realize that *Lā ilāha ill'Allāh*, that is to come to know that in the end there is only one Absolute Reality. It is to realize the absolute nature of Allah and the relativity of all else that is other than He. Moreover, it is only this truth which the intelligence can know in an absolute sense. Everything else it knows only relatively. Only this certainty belongs to the very nature of man. It is only this knowledge which man can attain with absolute certitude.

What is the nature of the will? It is to be able to choose, to choose freely between two alternatives, between the real and the unreal, between the true and the false, between the Absolute and the relative. Were man not to be free religion would have no real meaning. Free will is necessary to the religious conception of man and this is as much true of Islam as of any other religion. Let us here clear away one of most malicious misunderstandings about Islam, namely the belief that Islam is fatalistic in the popular sense of the word. The common conception of Islam in the Western world has in fact become more than anything else centred on this so-called fatalism in which human free will and initiative have no role. The truth of the matter is otherwise. Were Islam to be fatalistic it would not be able to conquer half the known world in seventy years. It is actually absurd to call one of the most virile, patriarchal and energetic civilizations which the world has known fatalistic.

What Islam does emphasize is complete confidence in God, reliance on His Will and the realization that only God is absolutely free because only He is infinite. But man by virtue of his theomorphic nature shares in this freedom of the will which really belongs to God. In an absolute sense only God is free because only He is absolutely real. But from the human point of view to the degree that man is real he is also free. This question is of course one of the most difficult to solve from the point of view of human reason, for the dichotomy between free will and determinism is one that transcends the domain of discursive thought and can only be comprehended through that intellectual intuition which alone can realize the *coincidentia oppositorum*. Its discussion has a long history in Christian and Jewish theology as well as in Islam. What is, however, emphasized in Islam is that freedom in an absolute sense belongs to God alone. Nevertheless, we share in this freedom and therefore bear the responsibility of having to choose. Were this responsibility not to be incumbent upon us there would be no real meaning to religious faith.

As for speech, it is the most direct manifestation of what we are, of our innermost being. We cannot express our being in any way more directly than in speech. Speech is in a sense the external form of what we are inwardly. Islam, therefore, makes it central in its rites which revolve most of all around prayer. The central rite of Islam which has been called the prop of religion (*rukn al-dīn*) is the daily prayers (*ṣalāt*) which in its ever recurring rhythm integrates man's life into a spiritual centre. In Sufism, moreover, prayer is *the* method of realization in the form of invocation (*dhikr*) or the 'prayer of the heart' that becomes ultimately integrated into the very rhythm of the most elemental process of life, namely the beating of the heart. Invocation is to be able to remember God by invoking His Name at all times and in a more external sense to use the power of speech as prayer.

Of course there is no religion in which prayer does not exist in one form or another, any more than there is a religion in which will and intelligence do not play a role. But the emphasis in

Islam which marks its particular spiritual genius is to make these three elements, that is, intelligence, will and speech, the basis of the spiritual life by penetrating to the essence of these elements and revealing their essential nature.

Islam poses the ultimate question 'what is intelligence and what does it really mean to be intelligent?' Intelligence is not what it has become so often in modern time, a mental acumen and diabolical cleverness which goes on playing with ideas endlessly without ever penetrating or realizing them. This is not real intelligence, not contemplative intelligence which differs as much from mental virtuosity as the soaring flight of an eagle differs from the play of a monkey. What we call intelligence today is precisely this monkey play of the mind which plays with ideas, were they even to be sacred ones, without ever being able fully to understand and penetrate any one of them. Such a mind is like a lake which has become frozen. Nothing ever penetrates into it; rather, everything glides from one side to the other leaving the deeper layers untouched. It is not this type of mental activity which Islam considers as intelligence, an activity which is at best no more than a reflection of true intelligence.

This is not the place to analyse fully the Arabic world *al-'aql* which means both reason and intellect and although used to mean reason is also what binds us to God. In fact one of the meanings of the root *'aql* is to tie or to bind. The Quran calls those who have gone astray from religion as those who cannot intellect, *'lā ya'qilūn'*, those who cannot use their intelligence correctly. It is very significant that the loss of faith is equated in Quranic language not with the corruption of the will but with the improper functioning of intelligence.

Herein lies one of the major distinctions between the Islamic and Christian points of view, one that makes it difficult for many Westerners to understand the nature of the Islamic perspective. Christianity is essentially a mystery which veils the Divine from man. The beauty of Christianity lies in the acceptance of God as a mystery and in bowing before this mystery, in believing in the unknown as St. Augustine said. In Islam, however, it is man who is veiled from God. The Divine Being is not veiled from us, we are veiled from Him and it is for us to try to rend this veil asunder, to try to know God. Our intelligence is not a Luciferian faculty but a God-given instrument whose ultimate object is God Himself. Islam is thus essentially a way of knowledge; it is a way of gnosis (*ma'rifah*). It is based on gnosis or direct knowledge that however cannot by any means be equated with rationalism which is only an indirect and secondary form of knowledge. Islam leads to that essential knowledge which integrates our being, which makes us know what we are and be what we know or in other words integrates knowledge and being in the ultimate unitive vision of Reality.

It might now be asked why then does man have need of revelation if he is a theomorphic being endowed with an intelligence which can lead him to a knowledge of God and affirmation of Unity (*tawḥīd*). This is a problem that needs much explanation especially since certain modern Muslim apologists, wanting to answer Christian charges against Islam and at the same time not being intellectually strong enough to state the case of Islam in its true perspective, have claimed that indeed Islam has no need of mysteries, miracles, original sin, and just about everything else which is 'supernatural' from the Christian point of view. Islam is presented as if its conception of man is the Cartesian rational man left to his own reason who, however, instead of becoming a deist or agnostic as in the West somehow becomes a Muslim. This view, however, is not at all true because although Islam is based on the primordial nature of man and his intelligence rather than will which has become warped after his fall on earth, it nevertheless believes that revelation is absolutely necessary. Without the aid of God man cannot discover by himself the way of salvation, the 'Straight Path'.

Man needs revelation because although a theomorphic being he is by nature negligent and forgetful; he is by nature imperfect. Therefore he needs to be reminded. Adam, the first man, was also the first of prophets. Prophecy is thus necessary for mankind and begins with the first man himself. As Adam needed prophecy so do all men who are his progeny. Man cannot alone uplift himself spiritually. He must be awakened from the dream of negligence by one who is already awake. Man is thus in need of a message from heaven and must follow a revelation in order to realize the full potentiality of his being and have the obstacles which bar the correct functioning of his intelligence removed. Intelligence does lead to God but provided it is wholesome and healthy (*salīm*), and it is precisely revelation, this objective manifestation of the Intellect, that guarantees this wholesomeness and permits the intelligence to function correctly and not be impeded by the passions. Every man needs to follow a prophet and a revelation unless he is himself chosen as a prophet or in certain other very exceptional cases which are only exceptions that prove the rule and demonstrate that 'the Spirit bloweth where it listeth'.

The most profound reason for the need of revelation is the presence of obstacles before the intelligence which prevent its correct functioning, or more directly the fact that although man is made in the 'image of God' and has a theomorphic being he is always in the process of forgetting it. He has in himself the possibility of being God-like but he is always in the state of neglecting this possibility. That is why the cardinal sin in Islam is forgetfulness. It is negligence (*ghaflah*) of what we really are. It is a going to sleep and creating a dream world around us which makes us forget who we really are and what we should be doing in this world. Revelation is there to awaken man from this dream and remind him what it really means to be man.

A man is not a man by the fact that he has two hands with which he manipulates or that he can make planes that fly or calculating machines that perform difficult mathematical operations in a short time. These and other abilities are no more than accidental to his real nature which makes of him a man for quite different reasons.

There is a story at the end of the epistle on animals in the *Rasā'il* (*Epistles*) of the Ikhwān al-Ṣafā' (Brethren of Purity) in which a dialogue is carried out between man and the animals. The members of the animal kingdom complain before the king of the jinn about man's cruelty to them, about how he uses them as beasts of burden, drinks their milk and eats their flesh and takes advantage of them in many other ways to fulfil his own need without considering the rights of the animal kingdom. Man is invited to answer the charges brought against him. He tries to prove his superiority by mentioning how he can build buildings and cities, calculate and manipulate numbers, create a complicated social structure, develop arts and science and many other skills of the kind. To each of these claims one of the members of the animal kingdom answers by pointing out to a corresponding skill possessed by one of the animal species like the bee who is a natural geometer and makes hexagons for his beehive. Every advantage which man enumerates for himself and thinks that thereby he has the right to dominate over nature and destroy it, as he has done with unprecedented ferocity during the past century, is thus overcome by the animals. It is only when man mentions that within human society there are saints who are God's representatives on earth, who are the channels of grace for the whole terrestrial environment, and who fulfil the very *raison d'être* of life on earth as such, that the animals bow before the claims of man to dominate over them. Man's central position in the world is not due to his cleverness or inventive genius but because of the possibility of attaining sanctity and becoming a channel of grace for the world about him.

This story demonstrates the Islamic conception of man according to which man participates fully in the human state, not through the many activities with which he usually identifies himself but by remembering his theomorphic nature. And because he is always in the process of forgetting this nature he is always in need of revelation. In Christianity man has sinned, having sinned his nature has become warped; it having become warped he needs a miracle to save him. Through baptism and the sacraments this wound in his soul is healed and by participation in the life and sacrifice of Christ he is saved. In Islam, however, there is no original sin. There is no single act which has warped and distorted human will. Rather, man by being man is imperfect, only God being perfection as such. Being imperfect man has the tendency to forget and so is in constant need of being reminded through revelation of his real nature. Therefore, although the starting point of the conception of man in Christianity and Islam is different the end result is in this sense the same, in that both believe in the necessity of revelation to save man.

Man is in absolute need of religion without which he is only accidentally human. It is only through participation in a tradition, that is, a divinely revealed way of living, thinking and being, that man really becomes man and is able to find meaning in life. It is only tradition in this sense that gives meaning to human existence. Many thinkers of the Enlightenment and the age of rationalism who theoretized against religion did not realize the profound need of man for religion or for meaning in an ultimate sense, and could not foresee that once deprived of a divinely revealed religion man, rather than becoming content, would begin to create pseudo-religions and the spiritually dangerous eclecticisms which have been showering mankind for the past century or two.

The privilege of participating in the human state, in a state which contains the opportunity and possibility of becoming God-like, of transcending the world of nature, and of possessing an immortal soul whose entelechy lies beyond the physical world, carries with it also a grave responsibility. This trust or responsibility of having the freedom to accept or reject faith is beautifully expressed in the Quranic verse: 'Lo! We offered the trust unto the heavens and the earth and the hills, but they shrank from bearing it and were afraid of it. And man assumed it. Lo! He hath proven a tyrant and a fool.' (XXXIII; 72) (انا عرضنا الامانة علی السموات والارض والجبال فابين ان يحملنها واشفقن منها وحملها الانسان انه كان ظلوماً جهولا.) The burden of responsibility of the human state was so great that neither the sky nor the mountains accepted to bear this heavy load. It was upon man's shoulders that this heavy responsibility was placed. As Hafez says, echoing the Quranic verse:

> For Heaven's self was all too weak to bear
> The burden of His love God laid on it.
> He turned to seek a messenger elsewhere
> And in the Book of Fate my name was writ.
>
> (Gertrude Bell translation).

آسمان بار امانت نتوانست کشید　　قرعهٔ فال بنام من دیوانه زدند

The very grandeur of the human condition is precisely in that he has both the possibility of reaching a state 'higher than the angels' and at the same time of denying God. Being given the possibility of being God-like through the acceptance of the 'trust of faith', man can also play the role of a little deity and deny God as such. Therein lies both the grandeur and seriousness of the human condition. Each being in the Universe is what it is. It is situated on a particular level of existence. Only man can stop being man. He can ascend above all degrees of universal existence and by the same token fall below the level of the basest of creatures. The alternatives of heaven and hell placed before man are themselves an indication of the seriousness of the human condition. Man is presented with a unique opportunity by being born in the human state and it is a tragedy for him to fret away and waste his life in pursuits which distract him from the essential goal of his life which is to save his immortal soul.

The supreme symbol of this trust, this precious burden which God has placed on the shoulders of man, a burden which if he bears safely grants him eternal felicity, is in Islam the black stone of the Ka'ba. There is in Mecca in the house of God a black stone which is in fact a meteor. In the Islamic tradition, this stone which fell from heaven, symbolizes the original covenant (*al-mīthāq*) made between man and God. God taught man the name of all the creatures as we are told in the Quran as well as in the Old Testament. This means that God gave man the possibility of dominating over all things for to possess the 'name' of a thing means to exercise power over it. Man has the right to breathe the air about him, to eat and drink to satiate his bodily desires, to walk upon the earth. None of these has man created himself. Man is moreover given life and a freedom to accept or deny the Creator Himself. This is in itself a miracle, a part of existence which can deny Being. We exist and yet there are men who deny Being, the source of all particular existence. Only men can become existentialists. Animals also exist but they are not existentialists.

It is itself a miracle that human existence is given the possibility of denying its own source. But man is given all this and much more in return for something which God wants of him and the black stone is the symbol of this covenant made between man and God. The idea of covenant is an aspect of religion often forgotten in modern times but it is essential in Islam and is of course strongly emphasized in the Old Testament. There, however, the covenant is made between God and a chosen people, the people of Israel, whereas in Islam it is made between God and man as such not a particular race or tribe.

Man by accepting the covenant has in turn certain duties to perform. He has, first of all, to make his intelligence conform to the Truth which comes from the Absolute, and then to make his will conform to the Will of the Absolute and his speech to what God wants of man. In brief, in return for all the blessings and gifts that God has given man, man must in turn remember his real nature and always keep before him the real goal of his terrestrial journey. He must know who he is and where he is going. This he can do only by conforming his intelligence to the Truth and his will to the Divine Law. A person who does not fulfil his religious obligations falls short in Muslim eyes on the simplest moral plane. He is like a man who has rented a house and refuses to pay the rent. Man has accepted a covenant with God but simply refuses to live up to his side of the agreement.

To accept the Divine covenant brings up the question of living according to the Divine Will. The very name of Islam is intimately connected with this cardinal idea. The root '*salama*' in Arabic, from which *Islam* is derived, has two meanings, one peace and the other surrender. He who surrenders himself to the Divine Will gains peace. The very idea of Islam is that through the use of intelligence which discerns between the Absolute and the relative one should come to surrender to the Will of the Absolute. This is the meaning of Muslim: one who has accepted through free choice to conform his will to the Divine Will.

In a particular sense Islam refers to the religion revealed through the Quran but in a more general sense it refers to religion as such. Some Muslim sages in fact see three different levels of meaning in the word 'Muslim'. Islam is actually like a several storied mountain and everything in it has different degrees and levels of meaning including the concept Muslim itself. Firstly, anyone who accepts a Divine revelation is a 'Muslim' in its most universal sense, be he a Muslim, Christian, Jew or Zoroastrian. The Islamic point of view did not take into account the Indian religions until historic contact was made with them but this definition would refer to them as well, as Hinduism came to be called by certain later Muslim sages the 'religion of Adam'. In its first meaning, therefore, Muslim refers to that human being who through the use of his intelligence and free will accepts a divinely revealed law.

Secondly, '*muslim*' refers to all creatures of the Universe who accept Divine law in the sense that they conform to the unbreakable laws which the Western world calls 'laws of Nature'. In modern times the very logical coherence of the natural world, its order and regularity, have turned many people away from a religious conception of nature as if the presence of God in Nature were manifested only through miracles. The fact that the sun rises regularly every morning and one observes no break in the regularity of the natural order was a major argument of eighteenth century and nineteenth century and even by modern rationalists against the Christian conception of the Universe. But this regularity proves in Muslim eyes just the opposite, namely the presence of the Divine Will to which all creatures are subservient and in fact, save for man, have no choice but to follow.

A stone has no choice but to fall. The force of gravitation is an expression of the Divine Will on the physical plane which the stone obeys absolutely so that in this sense it is '*muslim*'. It is the Will of the Creator that expresses itself in what is called 'laws of nature' in Western thought, and everything in the Universe is in a profound sense Muslim except for man who, because of this free choice given to him as a trust to bear, can refuse to submit to His Will. A tree grows and has no choice but to grow. Fire burns and cannot do otherwise. A pear tree must always bear pears. A tiger must always be a tiger and an eagle an eagle. A noble animal is always noble and a base one always base. It is only man who can be as ferocious as a tiger, as majestic as an eagle or lion, or as lowly as an earth worm. It is only man who can stop being a Muslim in this second meaning of the term '*muslim*', whereas all other beings are '*muslim*' in this sense by virtue of their complete submission to the Divine Will which manifests itself as 'laws of nature'.

Finally, there is the highest meaning of Muslim which applies to the saint. The saint is like nature in that every moment of his life is lived in conformity with the Divine Will, but his participation in the Divine Will is conscious and active whereas that of nature is passive. All beings in a sense know that they exist; only man knows that he knows and has a conscious knowledge of his own existence. It would perhaps be more logical to consider the first meaning of Muslim as pertaining to nature, the second meaning to man who has accepted a revelation, and the third meaning to the saint who not only has accepted revelation but lives fully in conformity with the Divine Will. As such the saint is the conscious, active and intellectual counterpart of the first kind of '*muslim*', that is, nature. Like nature he lives every moment of his life according to the Divine norm but consciously and with free will. He is thus the preserver of nature and its spiritual counterpart.

Islam is then a universal concept that comprehends man and the Universe about him and lies in the nature of things. Also in a more particular sense, as a religion which was revealed nearly fourteen hundred years ago, it continues to base itself on what is in the nature of things concentrating particularly on the Divine nature itself. For this reason Islam is based from beginning to end on the idea of Unity (*tawḥīd*), for God is One. Unity is the alpha and omega of Islam. It is, in fact, emphasized so much that for a non-Muslim it seems as a pleonasm, a kind of excessive reiteration of something which is obvious. But to the Muslim the idea of Unity does not just mean the assertion that there is only one God sitting in heaven instead of two or three. No religion could convert a quarter of the population of the globe and spread from Morocco to Indonesia with just such a simple idea. Such a concept would not be sufficient to attract men towards religion.

Unity is, in addition to a metaphysical assertion about the nature of the Absolute, a method of integration, a means of becoming whole and realizing the profound oneness of all existence. Every aspect of Islam rotates about the doctrine of Unity which Islam seeks to realize first of all in the human being in his inner and outward life. Every manifestation of human existence should be organically related to the *Shahādah, Lā ilāha ill'Allāh*, which is the most universal way of expressing Unity. This means that man should not be compartmentalized either in his thoughts or actions. Every action, even the manner of walking and eating, should manifest a spiritual norm which exists in his mind and heart.

On the social plane Unity expresses itself in the integration of human society which Islam has achieved to a remarkable degree. Politically it manifests itself in Islam's refusal to accept as the ultimate unit of the body politic anything less than the totality of the Islamic community, or the *ummah*. There is only one Muslim people, no matter how scattered and far removed its members may be. Only the complete *ummah* comprises that circle which is Islam and no segment of the Muslim community has a right to claim to be the *ummah* any more than a segment of a circle could claim circularity. The political ideal of a single Muslim government, with all the ups and downs it has experienced over the centuries, is based on the central metaphysical doctrine of Unity.

Unity also manifests itself in the realm of the arts and sciences, in which Islam cannot remain neutral *vis-à-vis* any form of knowledge. Islam has always sought to unify all domains of knowledge and therefore is faced with the particularly difficult problem of coming to grips with the actual discoveries and also the presumptions of modern science, a task which is not by any means solved by simply calling Islam 'scientific' as many modern Muslim apologists are prone to do. The problem is much more profound and delicate than that and Islam must face the same challenges that Christianity has faced since the seventeenth century. Moreover, Islam being essentially a way of knowledge must either answer any other form of science which claims to provide a knowledge of things or accept it. In any case its function is to integrate and the history of Islam has demonstrated this aspect of it in both philosophy and science as well as in art, in which forms were elucidated and elaborated to display Unity and no distinction has ever been made between the sacred and the profane.

Islam, in fact, being the religion of Unity has never distinguished between the spiritual and temporal or religious and profane in any domain. The very fact that there is not even a suitable word in Arabic, Persian or other Islamic languages for temporal or secular is the best indication that the corresponding concepts have not existed in Islam. Such a division does not exist because the kingdom of Caesar was never given unto Caesar in Islam. Being based on Unity Islam has envisaged a total way of life which excludes nothing. Its legislation is quite realistic in conformity with its perspective which is based on the real nature of things. It, therefore, envisages not only the saint but also the usual man with all his strengths and weaknesses. For this very reason it has been falsely accused by many Christians of being worldly or of being the religion of the sword.

This latter accusation is an important one which we must pause to answer. It is true that Islam has legislation for even war whereas Christianity orders man to turn the other cheek, and is mild and gentle in its teachings. But what is forgotten is that either a religion is made for saints, as Christ said, 'My Life is not of this world' in which case it leaves aside political, social and economic questions and envisages all of its followers as potential saints and, in fact, can only function in a society of saints. Or a religion tries to encompass the whole of man's life, in which case it must take into account the whole of man's nature with all the weaknesses and shortcomings it has, and legislate for the political and economic life of man as well as the purely religious aspect of his existence. Christianity certainly by addressing itself to the potential saint did not eliminate the non-saintly aspect of its followers, nor banish war from Christendom.

In fact the moment Christianity became the religion of a civilization and an empire it had to take the sword and fight in order to subsist. It had to choose between remaining the religion of monks or of a civilization which brought with it the responsibility of having to rule and fight wars. Such Christian kings as Charlemagne and St. Louis certainly fought as hard as any Muslim rulers. And to say the least the Christian warriors were not more gentle or generous than Muslims on the field of battle. Spain and Anatolia changed hands between Islam and Christianity about the same time. In Spain all the Muslims were either killed or driven off and no Muslims remain there today, whereas the seat of the Orthodox church is still located in Turkey.

The criticism against Islam as a religion of the sword is thus not a valid one. Islam by legislating war limited it, whereas Christianity left it outside its consideration. It is not accidental that the most devastating total wars of this century have begun in the West where Christianity has been the dominating religious influence. It used to be said by secularists that the wars fought between Christians and Muslims were due to religion and that religion is the cause of war. They did not know that the secularized modern world would kill more people in wars than religions ever did. War, in a limited sense at least, is actually in the nature of things and Islam, rather than leaving it aside as if it did not exist, limited it by accepting it and providing religious legislation for it. One can at least say that the terrible wars of this century have not come out of the Muslim world, but out of what some people have called the 'post-Christian' West. It is not to say that Christianity is to blame for them for they came from a society which had in many ways rebelled against Christianity. But not having a Divine Law to govern the external life of man as well as the spiritual domain, Christianity facilitated this secularization of political and social life and its divorce from revealed principles which in turn brought about the major upheavals of modern times.

It is not our aim by any means to criticize Christianity, but to defend Islam from this insidious charge made against it by many Westerners, especially a certain type of people who want to preserve a mediocre and empty way of life at all costs and believe that the role of religion is only in keeping peace to enable them to continue their mode of life and any religion which also deals with strife and war must be false. Actually a religion which seeks to encompass the whole of life must consider all of its realities. Life, like nature, has many facets; like nature it has lakes, flowers and fields which are peaceful and thunder and lightning which carry awe and power with them.

The revelation of the religious message itself is actually the opening of heaven to the human receptacle. Either it descends like lightning and leaves its effect rapidly or it flows like water and seeps in gradually. In both cases what exists before tumbles down and a new creation comes about. The Roman empire fell down with as much of a crash as the Persian empire. One was overcome spiritually by Christianity and the other by Islam. Christianity concentrating on man's spiritual life did not consider his political and social needs. Islam basing itself on Unity had to integrate all of human life and could not overlook any aspect of it. Only a false idealism could criticize the profound realism of Islam, which, instead of envisaging all men as saints and then having difficulty with the many who are far from the saintly life, bases itself on the real nature of man in both his spiritual and worldly aspirations which it tries to channel towards a spiritual direction by comprehending all things in its total scheme based on Unity.

This character of Islam is directly connected with the fact that it is both the 'primordial religion' and the last religion in the present life of humanity. Islam considers itself as the primordial religion (*al-dīn al-ḥanīf*) because it is based on the doctrine of Unity which has always existed and which lies in the nature of things. Every religion has been ultimately based on the doctrine of Unity so that in Islam it is said that 'the doctrine of Unity is unique' (*al-tawḥīd wāḥid*). There is only one doctrine of Unity which every religion has asserted and Islam came only to reaffirm what has always existed and thus to return to the primordial religion which was at the beginning and will always be, the eternal *sophia*, the *religio perennis*. It sought to accomplish this by its uncompromising emphasis upon Divine Unity and by seeking to return man to his original nature (*fiṭrah*) which is veiled from him because of his dream of negligence. According to the Islamic perspective God did not send different truths through His many prophets but different expressions and forms of the same fundamental truth of Unity. Islam is thus the reassertion of this primordial truth asserted in the cadre of the Abrahamic tradition in the climate of Semitic spirituality and using as a basis the three elements of intelligence, will and speech which make the realization of Unity possible.

In Islam there are three personalities who are similar, Adam, Abraham and the Prophet Muḥammad—upon whom be peace. The primordial religion based on Unity began with Adam himself. He was a 'monotheist' (*muwaḥḥid*) from the beginning. Mankind did not evolve gradually from polytheism to monotheism. On the contrary from time to time man deviated through religious decadence into polytheism from the original monotheism of the first man. Man was originally a monotheist who fell gradually into polytheism and has to be reminded periodically of the original doctrine of Unity. History consists of a series of cycles of decay and rejuvenation. Decay comes from the corrupting influences of the terrestrial environment, from the earth which pulls all things downwards and makes every spiritual force decay as it moves away gradually from its original source. Rejuvenation comes from heaven through the prophets who through successive revelations renew the religious and spiritual life of man. The Islamic conception of history is one of a series of cycles of prophecy, each cycle followed by a gradual decay leading to a new cycle or phase.

As Adam was the first man and prophet and at the beginning of man's terrestrial history, so does Abraham represent the reassertion of this role for the Semitic people. He symbolizes the unity of that tradition from which Judaism, Christianity and

Islam, the members of the 'Abrahamic community', issued forth. Being the 'father of monotheism' and the 'father of the Semites' he represents in Islam that primordial religion which Islam came to reassert. This universal message was later particularized for a 'chosen people' by Moses in the first separate religion to issue forth from the Abrahamic tradition. The revelation given to Moses was in fact the aspect of this tradition or for that matter the primordial religion as law so that Judaism came to emphasize the importance of following Divine Law, the 'Talmudic Law', as the basis of religion. The Divine Will was revealed in Judaism in the form of a concrete law according to which the daily life of man should be moulded.

Christ and the Christian revelation, on the other hand, represent the esoteric aspect of the Abrahamic tradition, the internal dimension of the primordial religion, which is a spiritual way rather than a law. Christ did not bring a new revealed law or *sharī'ah* but a way (*ṭarīqah*) based on the love of God. Islam recognized the particular function of Christ, which thus differed from that of other prophets who usually brought a law or reformed a previous one, by acknowledging his particular nature as the 'Spirit of God' (*rūḥ Allāh*) and his 'supernatural birth' connected with the virginity of Mary. 'And she who was chaste, therefore We breathed into her (something) of Our Spirit and made her and her son a token for (all) peoples.' (Quran XXI, 91)

(والتى احصنت فرجها فنفخنا فيها من روحنا وجعلناها وابنهآ ءاية للعالمين)

Also 'Verily the Messiah, Jesus the son of Mary, is but a Messenger of God, and His Word which He conveyed unto Mary, and a Spirit from Him' (IV 171)

(انما المسيح عيسى ابن مريم رسول الله وكلمته القاها الى مريم وروح منه)

Thus Christ continued to be seen in Islam as a prophet rather than as an incarnation. What Islam does not accept in Christianity is first of all the idea of filial relationship and secondly the Trinity as usually understood, both of which are alien to the Islamic perspective, because the latter is based on the nature of the Absolute itself and not on its manifestations or 'descents'. Putting these two points aside, Islam has a high regard for Christ who plays a particularly significant role in certain phases of Sufism.

Islam believes itself to be the third great manifestation of the

Abrahamic tradition, after Judaism and Christianity. Now, as Christians know so well trinity is a reflection of unity so that this third manifestation of the Abrahamic tradition is in a sense a return to the original Unity, to the 'religion of Abraham'. As Judaism represents the law or the exoteric aspect of this tradition and Christianity the way or the esoteric aspect of it, so does Islam integrate the tradition in its original unity by containing both a law and a way, a *sharī'ah* and a *ṭarīqah*. Moreover, it can be said that in a sense Judaism is essentially based on the fear of God, Christianity on the love of Him and Islam on the knowledge of Him although this is only a matter of emphasis, each integral religion containing of necessity all these three fundamental aspects of the relation between man and God.

If Islam is thus the 'primordial religion' it is also the 'last religion' and in fact it is through this particularity that it becomes not just religion as such but a particular religion to be accepted and followed. By re-affirming what all the prophets have asserted over the ages Islam emphasized its universal character as the primordial religion and by considering itself as the last religion, a claim by the way which in fact no other orthodox religion before Islam had ever made, Islam attained its particularity which distinguishes it and gives it its specific form as a religion. No religion can in fact be the universal religion as such. It is so inwardly, but outwardly it must be a particular religion which induces men to accept and follow it through specific forms and rites. Man living in the realm of the particular must begin from the particular in order to reach the universal. The beauty of revealed religion is precisely that although externally it is a form, it is not a closed form but one which opens inwardly towards the Infinite. It is a way from the particular to the universal provided one is willing to accept its form and follow it and not reject the form in the name of a universality which can only be reached through the penetration of forms that are a part of the revelation itself. Islam also had to have a particular form and that came from its character as the last religion. With the Prophet the prophetic cycle came to an end. The Prophet who was the 'Seal of Prophecy' (*khātam al anbiyā'*) announced that there would be no prophets after him and history has gone to prove his claim.

Of course such a conception of prophecy does not imply that mankind will go on forever without any other message from heaven. Islam does not envisage an indefinitely prolonged march of history for eons on end. It believes that the history of the present humanity has a beginning and an end marked by the eschatological events described in the Quran and *Ḥadīth*. It is until the occurrence of these events that no new prophet shall come and at the end of the cycle Islam believes, like Christianity, not in the coming of a new prophet but in the second coming of Christ. Until such a happening Islam is the last religion and the Prophet the last prophet not to be followed by another revelation from heaven.

This particularity of Islam as the last religion in the prophetic cycle gives it the power of synthesis so characteristic of this tradition. Being the final message of revelation Islam was given providentially the power to synthesize, to integrate and absorb whatever was in conformity with its perspective from previous civilizations. But this power of integration into Unity never meant a levelling out into uniformity which is the antipode of essential unity. Islam has never been a force for reducing things to a substantial and material uniformity but of integration which has preserved local features and characteristics while unifying them into its universal perspective. Islam integrated in its world-view what was ultimately in conformity with the *Shahādah, Lā ilāha ill'Allāh,* which is the final criterion of orthodoxy in Islam. Whatever did not negate the unity of the Divine Principle and the subsequent unicity of nature in either form or content was of interest to Islam and became often integrated into some of its intellectual perspectives.

Islam, thus took no interest in the Greek pantheon described by Homer and Hesiod but was deeply interested in the sapiential doctrines of the Pythagorean-Platonic as well as Aristotelian schools which affirmed Divine Unity. It likewise showed no interest in Zoroastrian dualism but certain schools such as the Illuminationist school of Suhrawardī integrated the Zoroastrian doctrine of angels into Islamic philosophy precisely because it was in conformity with the Islamic perspective and could be integrated into it.

Coming at the end of the prophetic cycle, Islam has considered all the wisdom of traditions before it as in a sense its own and has never been shy of borrowing from them and transforming them into elements of its own world view. Such a characteristic of Islam does not, however, mean in any way that Islam is unoriginal or does not possess its own spiritual genius, which is displayed in every manifestation of Islamic civilization. Today originality has come to mean being simply different even if it means to be wrong. Whereas in Islam, as in every orthodox tradition, originality means to express the universal truths that are perennial in a manner that is fresh and bears the fragrance of spirituality indicating that the expression comes not from outward imitation but from the source of the Truth itself.

Christianity accepted the decadent naturalistic Roman art which it found before itself and transformed it through its particular genius into a most powerful 'otherworldly' art, as the transformation of sculpture on sarcophagi of the fourth century A.D. demonstrates so clearly. It took Graeco-Roman philosophy with all the naturalism and rationalism inherent in its later schools and transformed it into a language for the expression of the mysteries of Christianity as seen in the writings of the early Church Fathers. This is true in fact of every living spiritual tradition which like a live organism accepts material from its surroundings and transforms it into what conforms to its own organic needs. Spiritual vitality, like organic, comes not in creation from nothing but in transformation and integration into a pattern which comes in essence from heaven. It is, therefore, surprising that so many modern Christian writers have denied the originality of Islam whereas every argument presented against Islam could be turned around and applied often with more force against Christianity itself. If one tries to deny the originality of a religious tradition by the fact that ideas and forms of previous traditions are present in it then Christianity not only adopted the Jewish religious perspective as well as Graeco-Roman art and philosophy but took over the institutions of law and government *in toto* from Roman civilization whereas Islam at least has had its own distinct law and social institutions. If any claims are made against originality in Islam, it might come from those who deny revelation as such, but surely it should not come with any logic from Christian quarters.

To summarize then, Islam is based on the universal relation

between God and man, God in His Absoluteness and man in his profound theomorphic nature. Islam bases the realization of this central relationship on intelligence, will and speech and consequently on equilibrium and certitude. It has sought to establish equilibrium in life by channelling all of man's natural needs and inclinations, all those natural desires and needs such as that for food, shelter, procreation, etc. given by God and necessary in human life, through the Divine Law or *Sharī'ah*. And upon the firm foundations of this equilibrium Islam has enabled man to build a spiritual castle based on contemplation and the certainty that there is no divinity other than the Absolute. In this sense its method is in contrast to Christianity in which love plays the central role and sacrifice is the outstanding virtue. For this very reason Christians have often criticized Islamic virtues as being mediocre and contributing simply to a social equilibrium whereas the Christian love of sacrifice seems to a Muslim as a kind of individualism which breaks the universal relationship between what is natural in man and the Divine Being. Yet, both the Islamic virtues leading to equilibrium which prepares the ground for contemplation and the Christian stress on love and sacrifice are means whereby man can escape the limited prison of his carnal soul and come to realize the lofty end for which he was put on earth.

Islam is a Divine revelation which was placed as a seed in the heart of man who was the receptacle of this Divine message. Man is the container. He cannot break this container; he can only purify it and empty it of the pungent substance that fills it so that it can become worthy of receiving the Divine nectar. It is by emptying the cup that man becomes worthy of receiving the message of heaven. It is by becoming a worthy field that the Divine seed becomes sown in it. The seed of Islam was placed in the heart of man through the Quran and the instrument of its propagation among men, the Prophet. From this seed there grew that spiritual tree which has created one of the greatest civilizations in history, a tree under whose shade a sizeable segment of the human race live and die today and find meaning and fulfilment in life.

Suggestions for further reading

Asad, M., *The Road to Mecca*, London, Reinhardt, 1954. An account of the experience of becoming a Muslim and living the religious life of Islam by a European convert to Islam who has had wide experience of the Muslim world.

Brohi, A. K., *Islam in the Modern World*, Karachi Islamic Research Academy, 1968. A collection of essays on various aspects of Islam and their application to the modern world by one of the leading Islamic thinkers of Pakistan.

Cragg, K., *Call of the Minaret*, London, Oxford University Press, 1956. A sympathetic study of Islam and a discussion of Muslim–Christian relations by one who has some first hand acquaintance with the Islamic way of life.

Dermenghem, E., *Muhammad and the Islamic Tradition*, trans. by J. M. Watt, New York, Harper, 1958. A useful textual and pictorial introduction to the Islamic tradition written with sympathy and understanding.

Esin, E., *Mecca the Blessed, Medinah the Radiant*, London, Paul Elek, 1963. The best modern pictorial study of the birthplace of Islam.

Gibb, H. A. R., "Islam", in *the Concise Encyclopaedia of Living Faiths*, ed. R. C. Zaehner, London, Hutchinson, 1959.

—*Muhammadanism*, New York, Oxford University Press, 1962. A very good summary of Islam especially Islamic law and institutions by one of the greatest Western authorities on Islamic studies.

Jameelah, M., *Islam in Theory and Practice*, Lahore, Muhammad Yusuf Khan, 1967. An uncompromising defense of Islam before the modern world with a rare sense of discernment and awareness of the real nature of the modern world by an American convert to Islam.

Jeffrey, A. (ed.), *A Reader on Islam*, S. Gravenhage, Moulton & Co. 1962., A selection of basic Islamic texts including the Quran and *Ḥadīth* translated into English with care and in a scholarly manner.

Mahmud, S. F., *The Story of Islam*, London, Oxford University Press, 1959. A general account of the whole of Islamic history by a contemporary Muslim author.

Massignon, L., *Opera Minora*, ed. Y. Moubarac, 3 vols., Beirut, Dar al-Maaref, 1963. Contains a series of illuminating studies on different aspects of Islam by one of the most penetrating and sympathetic of Western orientalists.

Maudoodi, S. A., trans. Kh. Ahmad, *Towards Understanding Islam*, Lahore, Islamic Publications, 1960. An exposition of Islam by a well-known modern Muslim scholar directed mostly towards the social, economic and political aspects of Islam.

Monteil, V., *Le Monde musulman*, Paris, Horizon de France, 1963. An excellent pictorial study of the whole of the Islamic world in all its geographical and ethnical diversity within the embracing unity of the faith.

Morgan, K. (ed.), *Islam, the Straight Path*, New York, Ronald Press, 1958. A collection of essays on different facets of Islam all written by modern Muslim scholars and authorities, ably edited, and well translated.

Nadwi, Abul Hasan Ali, trans. M. A. Kidwai, *The Four Pillars of Islam*, Lucknow, Academy of Islamic Research and Publications, 1972. The translation of a work of the well-known Indian *ʿālim* on the basic practices of Islam, namely the daily prayers, the religions tax, fasting and pilgrimage.

Padwick, C., *Muslim Devotions*, London, S.P.C.K., 1961. The best work in English on prayers which Muslims recite on all occasions of life, well chosen ând translated.

Schroeder, E., *Muhammad's People*, Portland, Bond Wheelwright, 1955. An outstanding authology of Islam and Islamic civilization written with much insight and understanding.

Schuon, F., *L'Oeil du coeur*, Paris, Gallimard, 1950, part one. Contains a profound discussion of Islamic angelology and the relation between the angelic world and revelation.

—*The Transcendent Unity of Religions*, trans. P. Townsend, New York, Pantheon, 1953, Chapters VI and VII. The most penetrating study of the relation between Islam and Christianity and Judaism as well as the Abrahamic religions and the religious traditions of the rest of Asia.

—*Understanding Islam*, trans. by D. M. Matheson, London, Allen & Unwin Co., 1963, Baltimore, Penguin Metaphysical Series, 1972, chapter I. The best work in English on the meaning of Islam and why Muslims believe in it, written from within and addressed primarily to Westerners and also those modernized Muslims who have become alienated from their own tradition.

Sharif, M. M. (ed.), *A History of Muslim Philosophy*, Vol. I, Wiesbaden, O. Harrassowitz, Book II, 1963. The first attempt made in the Islamic world to study the whole of Islam and its intellectual life from the Muslim point of view, including a study of the Islamic revelation itself.

Watt, W. Montgomery, *What is Islam?* London, Longmans, 1968. A summary of the author's well-known views on Islam.

CHAPTER II

The Quran
The Word of God, The Source of Knowledge and Action

The covenant made between man and God by virtue of which man accepted the trust (*amānah*) of being an intelligent and free being with all the opportunities and dangers that such a responsibility implies, is symbolized physically by the stone of the Ka'ba. Spiritually the record of this covenant is contained in the Quran, that central theophany of Islam which is itself the eloquent expression of this eternal covenant between God and man. In the Quranic verse 'Am I not your Lord' (VII, 172) (الست بربكم) God proposes to man even before the beginning of historical time and the creation of the earth this covenant and in answering 'Yea, we testify' (بلى شهدنا) man takes up the challenge of this invitation, and agrees to bear this trust as the 'servant of His Lord' (*'abd*). In this 'yea' lies the secret and the particular significance of human existence, of the life of this theomorphic being who is God's vicegerent or *khalīfah* on earth.

The Quran contains the message with the aid of which this covenant can be kept and the entelechy of human existence fulfilled. It is thus the central reality in the life of Islam. It is the world in which a Muslim lives. He is born with it inasmuch as the first sentence chanted in the ears of a newly born Muslim child is the *Shahādah* contained in the Quran. He learns certain sections of it as a child and begins to repeat some of its formulae from the moment he can speak. He reiterates some of its chapters in his daily prayers. He is married through sections read from the Sacred Book and when he dies the Quran is read for him. The Quran is the tissue out of which the life of a Muslim is woven; its sentences are like threads from which the substance of his soul is knit.

The Quran for the Muslim is the revelation of God and the book in which His message to man is contained. It is the Word of God revealed to the Prophet through the archangel Gabriel. The Prophet was therefore the instrument chosen by God for the revelation of His Word, of His Book of which both the spirit and the letter, the content and the form, are Divine. Not only the content and meaning comes from God but also the container and form which are thus an integral aspect of the revelation.

According to traditional sources, which alone matter in such questions, the Quran was revealed to the Prophet when he was spending some time, as he often did, in a cave in the mountain of Ḥirā' near Mecca. Suddenly the consciousness of the human receptacle was rent asunder by the archangel Gabriel, whose function in Islam is in many ways like that of the Holy Ghost in Christianity. He told the Prophet 'Recite!' (اقرأ) and with that word the descent of the Divine message began. It is of great significance that the first word of the Quran to be revealed was 'recite' for the supreme symbol of revelation in Islam is a book. In other religions the 'descent of the Absolute' has taken other forms, but in Islam as in other Semitic religions but with more emphasis, revelation is connected with a 'book' and in fact Islam envisages the followers of all revealed religions as 'people of the Book' (*ahl al-kitāb*).

To the command of Gabriel to 'recite' the Prophet answered by announcing that he did not have the ability to do so, being unlettered. But the Divine Message had itself given him the power to 'recite' the Book of God and henceforth he became the human recipient of this message which he made known to mankind. This religious truth, like many similar ones occurring in other traditions, is difficult for human reason to accept, not because it is itself illogical but because reason feeds upon daily sensible experience and is shocked by a phenomenon which transcends the bounds of that experience. One asks how could the Prophet be unlettered (*ummī*) and yet 'recite'. How could he be unlettered and yet announce the Quran which is the most beautiful of all works in the Arabic language, a book whose eloquence is itself the greatest miracle in Islam.

The Quran—the Word of God, the source of knowledge and action

Many Western authors writing about this cardinal question, begin with the assumption—often hidden in veils of so-called 'objectivity' and 'scholarship'—that the Quran is not really the Word of God, a revelation from heaven. Therefore, it must be explained away. Not being the Word of God, in their eyes it must naturally be the work of the Prophet who therefore must have been a very good poet and could not in fact have been unlettered. He must have learned bits here and there from the Jewish community in Medina or the Christian monks in Syria and put them together in a book that appears to these critics as a poor replica of other sacred books such as the Torah and the Gospels.

Such a view might be defended by one who rejects all revelation as such but it is strange to hear such views from authors who often accept Christianity and Judaism as revealed truth. It is enough to make a morphological comparison between Islam and let us say Christianity to realize why the Prophet must have been unlettered and why a man who understands religion metaphysically and intellectually must either accept religion as such, that is, all orthodox tradition, or be in the danger of either intellectual inconsistency or spiritual hypocrisy.

One could of course make a comparison between Islam and Christianity by comparing the Prophet to Christ, the Quran to The New Testament, Gabriel to The Holy Ghost, the Arabic language to Aramaic, the language spoken by Christ, etc. In this way the sacred book in one religion would correspond to the sacred book in the other religion, the central figure in one religion to the central figure in the other religion and so on. This type of comparison would be of course meaningful and reveal useful knowledge of the structure of the two religions. But in order to understand what the Quran means to Muslims and why the Prophet is believed to be unlettered according to Islamic belief, it is more significant to consider this comparison from another point of view.

The Word of God in Islam is the Quran; in Christianity it is Christ. The vehicle of the Divine Message in Christianity is the Virgin Mary; in Islam it is the soul of the Prophet. The Prophet must be unlettered for the same reason that the Virgin Mary must be virgin. The human vehicle of a Divine Message must be pure and untainted. The Divine Word can only be written on the pure and 'untouched' tablet of human receptivity. If this Word is in the form of flesh the purity is symbolized by the virginity of the mother who gives birth to the Word, and if it is in the form of a book this purity is symbolized by the unlettered nature of the person who is chosen to announce this Word among men. One could not with any logic reject the unlettered nature of the Prophet and in the same breath defend the virginity of Mary. Both symbolize a profound aspect of this mystery of revelation and once understood one cannot be accepted and the other rejected.

The unlettered nature of the Prophet demonstrates how the human recipient is completely passive before the Divine. Were this purity and virginity of the soul not to exist, the Divine Word would become in a sense tainted with purely human knowledge and not be presented to mankind in its pristine purity. The Prophet was purely passive in the face of the revelation he received from God. He added nothing to this revelation himself. He did not write a book but conveyed the Sacred Book to mankind.

To carry this analogy further one can point to the fact that the Quran, being the Word of God, therefore corresponds to Christ in Christianity and the form of this book, which like the content is determined by the dictum of heaven, corresponds in a sense to the body of Christ. The form of the Quran is the Arabic language which religiously speaking is as inseparable from the Quran as the body of Christ is from Christ Himself. Arabic is the sacred language of Islam, but not its only cultural and scientific language, for in this domain Persian has played a vital role in the eastern lands of the Islamic world from Persia to China. Arabic is sacred in the sense that it is an integral part of the Quranic revelation whose very sounds and utterances play a role in the ritual acts of Islam.

Of course Islam was not meant only for the Arabs and it is not necessary to know Arabic well to be a good Muslim. There have been many great Muslim saints who could hardly speak or read Arabic. But the formulae of the Quran read in prayers and acts of worship must be in the sacred language of Arabic which alone enables one to penetrate into the content and be transformed by the Divine presence and grace (*barakah*) of the Divine Book. That is why, although it is not at all necessary to know Arabic well to be a Muslim, it is necessary as a minimum to know the necessary Quranic verses which play so important a role in acts of worship. That is also why the Quran cannot be translated into any language for ritual purposes and why non-Arab Muslims have always cultivated the study of Arabic, not the spoken Arabic with which one is able to speak about daily matters, but the Quranic Arabic which forms a part of religious education throughout the Muslim world and which aids in reading and understanding the Book of God.

It is difficult for Westerners to understand the meaning of a sacred language and the function it performs in certain religions because in Christianity there is no sacred language. And for this very reason many modernized Muslims cannot understand this important matter either, whether they be non-Arab Muslims who try to substitute other Islamic languages for Arabic in the acts of worship or Arabs themselves who try to secularize Arabic. The latter take advantage of the fact that God chose it as a language of revelation meant not for the Arabs alone but for a large segment of humanity as such, and mistake the sacred role of Arabic in Islam with its supposed role in prevalent forms of ethnic and linguistic nationalism.

In order to understand the role of Arabic in Islam we must glance briefly at the other great religious traditions of the world. One sees immediately that there are two types of traditions: one which is based on the founder of the tradition who is thus considered as a 'Divine descent', incarnation or in Hindu terms *avātara*, who is himself the 'Word of God' and the message of Heaven. In such traditions there is no sacred language because the body or external form of the founder itself is the external form of the Word. For example, in Christianity, Christ himself is the Word of God and it does not matter whether one celebrates mass in Greek, Latin or for that matter Arabic or Persian to be able to participate in the 'blood and body' of Christ. Latin in the Catholic church is a liturgical language not a sacred one.

Or to take a situation outside of the Abrahamic traditions, in Buddhism, the Buddha himself is the *avātara* or 'incarnation'. The early Buddhist texts first appeared in Sanskrit. Later they were translated into Pali, Tamil, Tibetan, Chinese, Japanese and many other languages. One can be a perfectly good Buddhist and not know Sanskrit and read the religious texts let us say in Japanese. Here again the form of the 'Word' is not a language, since the 'Word' is not a book but a person. The form is rather the external aspect of the Buddha himself and we know that in Buddhism the very beauty of the Buddha images saves.

In contrast to these traditions which at least in this respect resemble each other, although Buddhism and Christianity differ profoundly in other ways, there are others in which the founder is not himself the message of Heaven, the Word of God, but he is the messenger of this Word. In fact this is the aspect under which Islam envisages all revelation so that the founder of a religion is called *rasūl;* literally one who brings a *risālah* or message from God. In such religions since the founder himself is not the Word and his external form is not directly the form of the Word there must be a sacred language which is inextricably connected to the content of the message and providentially chosen as its vehicle of expression. The very sounds and words of such a sacred language are parts of the revelation and play the same role in such religions as the body of Christ does in Christianity.

Again to cite some examples, one could mention Judaism and Islam and in a different climate Hinduism. Moses was a prophet who brought a message from heaven. This message has as its sacred language Hebrew. An orthodox Jew could write Jewish philosophy and theology in Arabic as Maimonides did, but he could not perform his rites or read the Torah ritually in anything but Hebrew. He could make a philological or philosophical analysis of the Torah in another language, let us say Greek as was done by Philo, but he could not participate in the 'Divine Presence' of the Book of God except through the sacred language of Judaism. In Hinduism one could read the Vedas a hundred times in Bengali, but again, in the religious rites, a Brahmin must chant the Vedas in Sanskrit. Sanskrit is the sacred language of Hinduism, but Buddhism, which also used Sanskrit at the beginning, is not dependent upon it in the same way. The same applies *mutatis mutandis* to Christianity *vis-à-vis* Hebrew or Aramaic.

In the light of this analysis it is perhaps easier to understand what the role of Arabic is in Islam. A Persian could become a great Muslim philosopher or scientist and write in Persian as has often been the case. Or in fact he can compose Sufi poetry in Persian which has also been done to such an extent that Sufi poetry in Persian is richer than in Arabic. A Turk could rule over millions of Muslim men as sultan, and yet not be able to speak any Arabic as was the case for many centuries. A Muslim of the Indian subcontinent could write on Islamic jurisprudence in Persian, as has in fact been done often, more than in Persia itself. All these cases are legitimate and in fact quite natural since the Arab speaking world is only a part of the Islamic world. But neither a Persian nor a Turk nor an Indian Muslim could participate in the *barakah* of the Holy Book and perform his rites as a Muslim if he were to use, let us say, Turkish or Persian in the daily prayers. The efficacy of canonical prayers, litanies, invocations, etc. is contained not only in the content but also in the very sounds and reverbrations of the sacred language. Religion is not philosophy or theology meant only for the mental plane. It is a method of integrating our whole being including the psychical and the corporeal. The sacred language serves precisely as a providential means whereby man can come not only to think about the truths of religion, which is only for people of a certain type of mentality, but to participate with his whole being in a Divine norm. This truth is universally applicable, and especially it is clearly demonstrated in the case of the Quran whose formulae and verses are guide posts for the life of the Muslim and whose continuous repetition provides a heavenly shelter for man in the turmoil of his earthly existence.

Many people, especially non-Muslims, who read the Quran for the first time are struck by what appears as a kind of incoherence from the human point of view. It is neither like a highly mystical text nor a manual of Aristotelian logic, though it contains both mysticism and logic. It is not just poetry although it contains the most powerful poetry. The text of the Quran reveals human language crushed by the power of the Divine Word. It is as if human language were scattered into a thousand fragments like a wave scattered into drops against the rocks at sea. One feels through the shattering effect left upon the language of the Quran, the power of the Divine whence it originated. The Quran displays human language with all the weakness inherent in it becoming suddenly the recipient of the Divine Word and displaying its frailty before a power which is infinitely greater than man can imagine.

The Quran, like every sacred text, should not be compared with any form of human writing because precisely it is a Divine message in human language. This fact holds true for the Bible as well, which we must recall includes not only the Gospels but also the Old Testament and the Book of the Apocalypse. There one sees, as in the Quran, an element which appears incoherent. Yet, it is not the sacred text that is incoherent. It is man himself who is incoherent and it takes much effort for him to integrate himself into his Centre so that the message of the Divine book will become clarified for him and reveal to him its inner meaning.

The whole difficulty in reading the Quran and trying to reach its meaning is the incommensurability between the Divine message and the human recipient, between what God speaks and what man can hear in a language which despite its being a sacred language is, nevertheless, a language of men. But it is a sacred language because God has chosen it as His instrument of communication, and He always chooses to 'speak' in a language which is primordial and which expresses the profoundest truths in the most concrete terms. It is only later that the sacred language develops an abstract and philosophical dimension. A sacred language is profound in depth and usually little developed on the surface as can be seen in Quranic Arabic. Every word carries a world of meaning within itself and there is never a complete 'horizontal' and didactic explanation of its content.

Yet, the Quran contains different types of chapters and verses within itself, some of which are didactic and explanatory, although not in an exhaustive sense, and others poetic, usually short and to the point. The Quran is composed of a profusion and intertwining of plant life as seen in a forest often combined suddenly with the geometry, symmetry and clarity of the mineral kingdom, of a crystal held before light. The key to Islamic art is in fact this combination of plant and mineral forms as inspired by the form of expression of the Quran which displays this character clearly. Some verses or chapters are extended like arabesques which became later formalized in the corporeal world as decoration of mosques combined with the actual verses of the Quran. Others are sudden bursts of a very clear and pointed idea expressed in a language which is much more geometric and symmetrical as seen particularly in the later chapters of the Sacred Book.

Now, the power of the Quran does not lie in that it expresses a historical fact or phenomenon. It lies in that it is a symbol whose meaning is valid always because it concerns not a particular fact in a particular time but truths which being in the very nature of things are perennial. Of course the Quran does mention certain facts such as the rebellion of a certain people against God and His punishment of those people as we see also in the Old Testament. But even those 'facts' retain their power because they concern us as symbols of a reality which is always present. The miracle of the Quran lies in its possessing a language which has the efficacy of moving the souls of men now, nearly fourteen hundred years since it was revealed, as much as it did at the beginning of its appearance on earth. A Muslim is moved by the very sound of the Quran and it is said that a test of a person's faith (*īmān*) is whether he is moved by the daily calls to prayer (*adhān*) and the chanting of the Quran or not. This power lies precisely in its nature as symbol not fact, as the symbol of a truth which concerns man vitally here and now.

The Quran actually bears three names in traditional Islamic sources which cast light upon its nature and constitution. The Sacred Book of Islam is first *al-Qur'ān*, then *al-Furqān*, and finally *Umm al-kitāb*. The Book is first of all *al-Qur'ān*, namely a recitation from which its common name is derived. It is also *al-Furqān*, that is a discernment, a discrimination; and finally it is *Umm al-kitāb*, the mother of all books. In these three appellations one finds the profound significance of this Book for Islam. It is a recitation in the sense that it is a means of concentration upon the truth for 'recitation' is a concentration in which ideas and thoughts are directed towards the expression of a certain end. As such the Quran is an assemblage of 'ideas' and 'thoughts' leading towards a concentration upon the truth contained in them. It is also a *furqān* or discrimination in that it is *the* instrument by which man can come to discriminate between Truth and falsehood, to discern between the Real and the unreal, the Absolute and the relative, the good and the evil, the beautiful and the ugly.

Finally as the 'Mother of books' the Quran is the prototype of all 'books', that is, of all knowledge. From the Islamic point of view all knowledge is contained in essence in the Quran, the knowledge of all orders of reality. But this knowledge lies within the Quran potentially, or as a seed and in principle, not actually. The Quran contains the principles of all science but does not seek to tell us the number of plants found in a particular continent or the number of elements that exist in the chemical table. It is useless and in fact absurd to try to find detailed scientific information in the Quran as has been done by certain modern commentators of it, as meaningless as the attempt made in the West to correlate scientific discoveries with the text of the Bible. By the time one comes to correlate the findings of a particular science with the text of the Holy Book, that science itself has changed and one is faced with the embarrassing situation of having correlated an eternal message with a transient form of knowledge which, in fact, is no longer held to be true. What the Quran does contain is the principle of all knowledge, including cosmology and the sciences of nature. But to understand these principles one needs to penetrate into the meaning of the 'Mother of Books' and then discover what is the ground and foundation of the sciences, not their detailed content.

The Quran is then the source of knowledge in Islam not only metaphysically and religiously but even in the domain of particular fields of knowledge. Its role even in the development of Islamic philosophy and science has been considerable, though often neglected by modern scholars, to say nothing of the metaphysical, moral and juridical sciences. It has been the guide as well as the *cadre* in which all Muslim intellectual effort has taken place.

The Quran contains essentially three types of message for man. Firstly, it contains a doctrinal message, a set of doctrines which expound knowledge of the structure of reality and man's position in it. As such it contains a set of moral and juridical injunctions which is the basis of the Muslim Sacred Law or *Sharī'ah* and which concerns the life of man in every detail. It also contains metaphysics about the nature of the Godhead, a cosmology concerning the structure of the Universe and the multiple states of being, and an eschatology about man's final end and the hereafter. It contains a doctrine about human life, about history, about existence as such and its meaning. It bears all the teachings necessary for man to know who he is, where he is and where he should be going. It is thus the foundation of both Divine Law and metaphysical knowledge.

Secondly, the Quran contains a message which on the surface at least is like that of a vast book of history. It recounts the story of peoples, tribes, kings, prophets and saints over the ages, of their trials and tribulations. This message is essentially one couched in historical terms but addressed to the human soul. It depicts in vivid terms the ups and downs, the trials and vicissitudes of the human soul in terms of accounts of bygone people which were not only true about such and such a people and time but concern the soul here and now.

Were the Quran to concern only a tribe that went astray in Arabia, centuries before the birth of Christ, it would not be able to attract us and appear to us as possessing pertinence and actuality. But every event recounted about every being, every tribe, every race bears an essential meaning which concerns us. The hypocrite (*munāfiq*) who divides people and spreads falsehood in matters concerning religion also exists within the soul of every man, as does the person who has gone astray, or he who follows the 'Straight Path', or he who is punished by God or rewarded by Him. All the actors on the stage of sacred history as accounted in the Quran are also symbols of forces existing within the soul of man. The Quran, is, therefore, a vast commentary on man's terrestrial existence. It is a book whose reading reveals the significance of human life which begins with birth and ends with death, begins from God and returns to Him.

Thirdly, the Quran contains a quality which is difficult to express in modern language. One might call it a divine magic, if one understands this phrase metaphysically and not literally. The formulae of the Quran, because they come from God, have a power which is not identical with what we learn from them rationally by simply reading and reciting them. They are rather like a talisman which protects and guides man. That is why even the physical presence of the Quran carries a great grace or *barakah* with it. When a Muslim is in difficulty he reads certain verses of the Quran which pacify and comfort him. And when he wants something or is in dire need again he turns to appropriate verses from the Quran. Or again when a Muslim greets another, whether it be in the Hindu Kush or the Atlas mountains, he uses the formula of *salām* drawn from the Quran. All these words, phrases and sentences possess a divine magic which is connected with the presence of the Divine in the sacred language He has chosen to reveal His Word. In fact the power of the sacred formula or phrase exists also in other traditions having a sacred language, but not in religions where such a language is absent—at least not in the same way. Here the lack of such means of support is compensated for by the presence of icons, sacred iconographies and symbols which contain the 'Divine magic' within them.

On the level of practice, the most difficult aspect of Christianity for a Muslim to understand is the significance of the cross. Generally, a Muslim cannot understand why a Christian bows before the cross, carries it and in moments of distress makes the sign of the cross. From the other side Christians face the same difficulty *vis-à-vis* this 'magical' aspect of the Quran which Muslims carry with them and recite to gain support and protection.

The Quran possesses precisely a *barakah* for believers which is impossible to explain or analyse logically. But because of this Divine presence and *barakah* it endures from generation to generation. People read and memorize it by heart; they chant it and recite it from day to day and there have even been saints who have spent their whole life only in chanting the Quran. That is because the Divine presence in the text provides food for the souls of men. It is in fact a sacred act to recite the Quran. Its reading is a ritual act which God wishes man to perform over and over again throughout his earthly journey.

To write the Quran in Islam is like drawing an icon in Christianity. The early Christian saints, especially those of the Orthodox church, painted icons after years of asceticism and spiritual practice and in fact it is always an icon of this kind, not the naturalistic representations of Christ and the Virgin Mary from the Renaissance and later periods, that is attributed with miraculous power to heal and to answer the calls of men. In Islam also the writing of the Quran is such a sacred act and many a devout believer and even saint has also been a calligrapher who has performed a religious function in writing the text of the Sacred Book.

Taken as a whole the Quran is like existence itself, like the Universe and the beings who move through it. It contains all the elements of universal existence and for this reason is in itself a universe in which a Muslim places his life from beginning to end. Being composed of words, the 'composition' of the Quran leads naturally to the symbolism of the Pen and the Tablet that is so well known in Islam. Just as a written work is composed by writing with a pen on a tablet or paper so did God 'write' the eternal Quran by the Pen (*qalam*) which symbolizes the Universal Intellect upon the Guarded Tablet (*al-lawḥ al-maḥfūẓ*), the symbol of the substantial, material and passive pole of cosmic manifestation.

According to many *Hadīths*, God also 'wrote' the inner reality of all things on the Guarded Tablet before the creation of the world, a symbolism which has played an important role in Islamic cosmology. The Pen symbolizes the Word, the Logos, the Intellect, and the Tablet Universal substance, so that it can also be asserted from this point of view that 'It is by the Word that all things are made'. In a metaphysical sense, then, the Quran contains the prototype of all creation. It is the pattern upon which things were made. That is why in Islam one distinguishes between a Quran that is 'written' and 'composed' (*tadwīnī*), and a Quran which is 'ontological' and pertains to cosmic existence (*takwīnī*). This is not to say that there are two Qurans but that, metaphysically, the Quran has an aspect of knowledge connected with its text as a book and an aspect of being connected with its inner nature as the archetypical blueprint of the Universe.

In a less metaphysical and more practical sense, the Quran corresponds to the world we live in from day to day. Man lives in a world of multiplicity and before he becomes spiritually transformed, he is profoundly attached to this multiplicity. The roots of his soul are deeply sunk into the soil of this world. That is why he loves this world and finds it so difficult to detach himself from it and attach himself to God. There are only a few contemplatives in each society. For the vast majority of men there is need of things, of multiplicity, because their souls are divided in a thousand and one ways and nourished upon this multiplicity. It is multiplicity in which man lives and which he loves to such an extent that were he to be deprived of this world of multiplicity it would be like death for him. And in fact what is death spiritually but being removed from this multiplicity and brought back to Unity.

The Quran, being like a world, is also a multiplicity in its chapters and verses, words and letters. It is made of a world of ideas and formulae. But there is a great difference between this world of the Quran and the world as such. And herein lies the particular genius of the Quran. It tries to catch the soul in its own game. It begins by playing the game of the soul, the game of presenting a facade of multiplicity and diversity to which the soul is accustomed. The soul in first encountering it discovers the same differentiation and multiplicity to which it is accustomed through its experience with the world. But within the Quran is contained a peace, harmony and unity which is the very opposite of the effect of the world as such on the souls of men. The external multiplicity of the world is such that in it man runs from one thing to another without ever finding peace and contentment. His soul runs from one object of desire to another thinking that it will find contentment just around the corner. Yet, it is a corner which he somehow never reaches.

The Quran begins by also presenting to the soul the possibility of running from one 'thing' to another, of running around corners, of living in multiplicity, but within lies a peace and contentment which leaves the very opposite effect on the soul. Some of the Muslim sages have compared the Quran to a net with which God catches fish, that is, human souls. He plays the game of the fish, who like to swim about from one place to another and who cannot be still, but He places a net before them into which they run and in which they are caught through this very process of moving from one place to another. The Divine net is placed before them for their own benefit and well-being which they, however, may not realize at the time. The Quran does present itself as the world but a world in which there is not differentiation and dissipation but essentially integration and unification.

From another point of view complimentary to the above one, the Quran is the cosmos, the vast world of creation in which man lives and breathes. It is not accidental that the verses of the Quran as well as phenomena in nature and events within the soul of man are called signs or portents (*āyāt*). According to the well-known Quranic verse: 'We shall show them our portents on the horizons and within themselves until it will be manifest unto them that it is the Truth' (XLI, 53) (سنريهم آياتنا فى الآفاق وفى انفسهم حتى يتبين لهم انه الحق). God displays His 'signs', the *vestigia Dei*, on the horizons, that is, the cosmos and more specifically the world of nature and within the souls of man until man comes to realize that it is the Truth.

It is precisely these signs which are displayed in the Quran. This correspondence between the verses of the Quran and the phenomena of nature is essential in determining the Muslim conception of nature and charting the course of Islamic science. The Quran corresponds in a sense to nature, to God's creation. That is why when a Muslim looks at a natural phenomenon he should be reminded of God and His Power and Wisdom. Man should be reminded of the 'wonders of creation' and constantly see the 'signs' of God upon the horizons. This attitude which is one of the essential traits of Islam is inextricably tied to the correspondence between the Quran and the Universe.

Moreover, human experience is based on a world and a subject that lives in this world and travels through it. Man's existence can be analysed in terms of two realities, a world, a background, an environment, and a being, a traveller, who journeys through this background and lives in this environment. However one wishes to depict this reality—and nowhere is it better depicted visually than in Chinese landscape paintings which show a vast world of nature through which a physically minute traveller is passing—this fundamental distinction between the traveller and the world through which he passes remains. It is the basis of every human experience, whether it be physical, psychological or religious.

The Quran again reflects this reality. The chapters of the Book are like worlds and we who read them like the traveller journeying through them. Or from another point of view the chapters are like the worlds, or realms, and the verses like the subject passing through them. In this aspect as in so many other essential ones the Quran corresponds to the very structure of reality; it corresponds in its external and inward aspects to all degrees of reality and knowledge, of being and intellection, whether it be practical or theoretical, concerned with social and active life or with metaphysical knowledge and the contemplative life.

In fact besides containing the basis of the Divine Law, the Quran expounds also a metaphsyics, a cosmology and an eschatology whose expression and formulation is what it should be. Westerners have sometimes criticized the Quranic formulation in these matters, especially what pertains to the description of Paradise and Hell as being too 'sensual'. They perhaps labour too much under the classical prejudice of considering only the mental aspect of man and cannot understand the profound symbolism of the description involved. The Quranic description of Paradise which includes not only houris but quite significantly elements of nature especially birds, trees, flowers, and minerals is all that it need be. Either one is among simple believers who in this life also live in the world of the senses and are not concerned with the joys of contemplation in which case the description of Paradise and also Hell present to them, although in a summary fashion characteristic of all monotheistic religions, in definitive terms the possibilities which lies before man. Or he is a contemplative and prone to metaphysical speculation, in which case the Quranic description presents the profoundest possible expression of the after life in the concretest of languages which is that of symbolism.

In this case the sapiential traditional commentaries which have explained the symbolism involved and have also expanded the compressed formulation of the Quran to explain the intermediate states and the posthumous becoming of the soul provide enough intellectual substance for the greatest of theologians and metaphysicians. In this as in other cases the Quran is meant for both the simple peasant and the metaphysician and seer and of necessity contains levels of meaning for all types of believers. It is meaningless to criticize it because one cannot either accept its literal description or understand the profound symbolism involved.

Some may object at this point that the reading of the Quran reveals none of what has been mentioned, and that it is simply an account of wars, commands and restraints, and the description of reward and punishment in the after life. Many people in fact who read the Sacred Book receive no more from it than the literal message. This is because no sacred text opens itself to human scrutiny and reveals its secret so easily. The Quran is like the Universe with many planes of existence and levels of meaning. One has to be prepared to be able to penetrate its meaning. It is, moreover, particularly in the inspired commentaries, based on the clarification afforded by the *Ḥadīth* and written by those who have lived in the tradition and are qualified in the true sense to write commentaries, that man comes to understand explicitly and in more extended form what is contained often implicitly and in a contracted form in the Quran.

The same holds true in fact in other traditions. The Torah, for example does not explicitly contain Talmudic Law which is based on the sacred commentaries written upon the Torah. In Hinduism also most of the traditional sciences are based on the commentaries of the later sages upon the Vedas. Likewise, the inner meaning of the Quran can be understood, but for certain exceptional cases, only through the inspired commentaries each of which seeks to elucidate and elaborate certain aspects of the Book. These commentaries, however, have nothing to do with the so-called higher criticism which during this century has become an almost diabolical distortion of Sacred Scripture, making it a kind of second rate handbook of archaeology which one tries to understand through sheer historical methods rather than trying to penetrate inwardly into the meaning of the symbolism involved.

The Quranic commentary under discussion here is not at all an attempt to reduce the text to history. It is hermeneutic exegesis in the real sense of the term as it existed in early and medieval Christianity, in Judaism and in fact in every orthodox tradition possessing a sacred scripture. This type of commentary which is a penetration into the inner meaning of a sacred text is written by a traditional authority who has himself penetrated into the inner dimensions of his own being. Man sees in the sacred scriptures what he is himself, and the type of knowledge he can derive from the text depends precisely on 'who' he is.

It is apt to quote here a passage concerning the inner meaning of the Quran by Mawlānā Jalāl al-Dīn Rūmī, whose *Mathnawī* is itself a commentary in Persian verse upon the Quran. He writes in his *Fīhi mā fīhi* or *Discourses* (Arberry translation, London, 1961, pp. 236–237):

'The Koran is as a bride who does not disclose her face to you, for all that you draw aside the veil. That you should examine it, and yet not attain happiness and unveiling, is due to the fact that the act of drawing aside the veil has itself repulsed and tricked you, so that the bride has shown herself to you as ugly, as if to say, "I am not that beauty". The Koran is able to show itself in whatever form it pleases. But if you do not draw aside the veil and seek only its good pleasure, watering its sown field and attending on it from afar, toiling upon that which pleases it best, it will show its face to you without your drawing aside the veil.'

It is essential to realize that we cannot reach the inner meaning of the Quran until we ourselves have penetrated into the deeper dimensions of our being and also by the grace of heaven. If we approach the Quran superficially and are ourselves superficial beings floating on the surface of our existence and unaware of our profound roots, then the Quran appears to us also as having only a surface meaning. It hides its mysteries from us and we are not able to penetrate it. It is by spiritual travail that man is able to penetrate into the inner meaning of the sacred text, by that process which is called *ta'wīl* or symbolic and hermeneutic interpretation, just as *tafsīr* is the explanation of the external aspect of the Book.

The Arabic term *ta'wīl* contains etymologically the meaning of the process involved. It means literally to take something back to its beginning or origin. To penetrate into the inner mysteries of the Quran *is* precisely to reach back to its Origin because the Origin is the most inward, and the revelation or manifestation of the sacred text is at once a descent and an exteriorization of it. Everything actually comes from within to the outside, from the interior to the exterior and we who live 'in the exterior' must return to the interior if we are to reach the Origin. Everything has an interior (*bāṭin*) and an exterior (*ẓāhir*), and *ta'wīl* is to go from the *ẓāhir* to the *bāṭin*, from the external form to the inner meaning. The word phenomenon itself brings up the question 'of what', which implies the existence of a noumenon. Even Kant conceded the necessity of noumena but because he limited the intellect to reason he denied the possibility of our coming to know them. But when intellectual intuition is present and under the guidance of revelation one can penetrate the appearance to that reality of which the appearance is an appearance, one can journey from the exterior to the interior by this process of *ta'wīl*, which in the case of the Quran means coming to understand its inner message.

The idea of penetrating into the inner meaning of things is to be seen everywhere in Islam, in religion, philosophy, science and art. But it is particularly in the case of the Quran that *ta'wīl* is applied especially by the Sufis and the Shi'ah. To demonstrate the traditional basis of this important doctrine we quote two traditions, one from a Sunni and the other from a Shi'ite source. There is a famous tradition of the sixth Shi'ite Imam Ja'far al-Ṣādiq as follows: 'The Book of God contains four things: the announced expression (*'ibārah*), the allusion (*ishārah*), the hidden meaning related to the suprasensible worlds (*laṭā'if*), and the spiritual truths (*ḥaqā'iq*). The literary expression is for the common people (*'awāmm*); the allusion is for the elite (*khawāṣṣ*); the hidden meaning is for the friends of God (or saints) (*awliyā'*); and the spiritual truths are for the prophets (*anbiyā'*).

There is also a reference to the Prophet transmitted by Ibn 'Abbās, one of the most respected of transmitters of *Ḥadīth* in Sunni sources, as follows: One day while standing on Mt. 'Arafāt he made an allusion to the verse 'Allah it is who hath created seven heavens, and of the earth the like thereof' (LXV, 12) (الله الذى خلق سبع سموات و من الارض مثلهن) and turned to the people saying 'O men! if I were to comment before you this verse as I heard it commented upon by the Prophet himself you would stone me.' What does this statement mean but that there is an inner meaning to the Quran not meant for anyone except those who are qualified to hear and understand it.

The story of Moses and Khiḍr itself, elaborated in many later traditional sources, such as the *Mathnawī*, refers to the presence of an inner meaning in the Quran. Khidr, who is equivalent to Elias in the Judaeo-Christian tradition, symbolizes esotericism in Islam and Moses, the exoteric law. Khiḍr accepts to take Moses on a journey with him, provided he does not question what he does. Yet, his actions which appear on the surface to be meaningless and harmful and which include tearing down a wall and boring a hole in a ship are finally opposed outright by Moses. Hearing his opposition Khiḍr decides to discontinue the journey with Moses but explains before departing how each act performed was for a hidden purpose of which Moses was ignorant. Seeing the surface of events he judged them to be wrong but once their inner nature was revealed their validity became clear. Esotericism cannot be judged by exoteric standards, it has its own logic which no external approach can ever hope to master.

This is exactly the case with the Quran. It possesses an inner dimension which no amount of literal and philological analysis can reveal. And it is precisely this aspect of the Quran that is least known to the outside world. In the Islamic world itself, however, a long tradition of hermeneutic commentary upon the Quran exists, among the Sufis and in Shī'ism. Sufi commentaries upon the Sacred Book which are best known include that of Rūzbahān Baqlī Shīrāzī, Shams al-Dīn Mībudī, and the celebrated *Ta'wīl al-qur'ān* attributed to Ibn 'Arabī but actually by his Persian commentator, 'Abd al-Razzāq Kāshānī. The *Mathnawī* of Rūmī is also in every sense a commentary upon the Quran in Persian poetry. As for well-known Shī'ite commentaries which possess a theosophic and esoteric nature, they include: the commentaries of Ṣadr al-Dīn Shīrāzī and Sayyid Aḥmad 'Alawī on different chapters of the Quran, the *Mir'āt al-anwār* of Abu'l-Ḥasan Iṣfahānī which summarizes the whole Shī'ite approach to Quranic commentary and the monumental *al-Mīzān* by the contemporary master Sayyid Muḥammad Ḥusain Ṭabāṭabā'ī.

Besides these works in which the inner *sapientia* of the Sacred Book is revealed and made the basis and fountain of all knowledge, there are a number of Quranic commentaries written by theologians and philologists such as Fakhr al-Dīn al-Rāzī and Zamakhsharī and also by many of the Muslim philosophers which have hitherto been little studied. The significance of this latter category of works lies in that precisely here the conjunction between faith and reason, the harmony between religion and philosophy, was sought. Quranic commentary was the meeting ground for the knowledge derived from science and from the tenets of revelation. With the numerous works written on Ibn Sīnā in European languages as yet no thorough study has been made of his many commentaries upon various verses of the Quran where more than anywhere else he sought to harmonize faith and reason.

The whole process of penetrating the inner meaning of the Quran, of discovering that wisdom which alone is the common ground between religion and science, is based on this process of *ta'wīl*, which does not mean seeking after a metaphorical meaning or reading into the text. *Ta'wīl* for Sufism, or Shi'ism, does not possess the same meaning as it does in Mu'tazilite theology and in jurisprudence. It has nothing to do with the debate between the Ash'arites and Mu'tazilites over the literal meaning of the Quran versus rational interpretation of it. *Ta'wīl* in the sense used by the Sufis and Shi'ite sages is the penetration into the symbolic—and not allegorical—meaning of the text which is not a human interpretation but reaching a divinely pre-disposed sense placed within the Sacred Text through which man himself becomes transformed. The symbol has an ontological reality that lies above any mental constructions. Man does not make symbols. He is transformed by them. And it is as such that the Quran with the worlds of meaning that lie hidden in its every phrase transforms and remakes the soul of man.

In fact, as pointed out already, not only do the teachings of the Quran direct the life of a Muslim, but what is more the soul of a Muslim is like a mosaic made up of formulae of the Quran in which he breathes and lives. Some of these formulae are so common and yet profound that their meaning must be analysed in order to understand the most elemental attitude of the Muslim towards life as determined by the Quran. The most fundamental formula of the Quran is the first *Shahādah*, that is, witness or testimony, *Lā ilāha ill'Allāh*, which is the fountain head of all Islamic doctrine, the alpha and omega of the Islamic message. In it is contained all of metaphysics. He who knows it knows everything in principle. It is both the doctrine and the method, the doctrine because it negates all relativity and multiplicity from the Absolute and returns all positive qualities back to God, the method because it is the means whereby the soul can combat against the enemies within. The very *lā* at the beginning is a sword—and in Arabic calligraphy the *lām* in fact resembles a sword—by which the soul is able to kill all the evil tendencies within itself which prevent it from becoming unified and which endanger it towards polytheism, or *shirk*, by making it see the relative as Absolute. A Muslim repeats the *Shahādah*, not only because it reaffirms over and over again Divine Unity but also because, through its repetition, this Unity comes to leave its permanent imprint upon the human soul and integrates it into its Centre. It is a sword with which the 'deities' that keep springing up in the soul are destroyed and all multiplicity and otherness is negated.

After the *Shahādah* the most cardinal and often used formula is *Bismillāh al-raḥmān al-raḥīm*, which is usually translated as in the Name of God, the Most Merciful and Compassionate but which could also be rendered as in the Name of God, the Infinitely Good, and the ever Merciful. The formula begins with the name *Allāh* followed by the two Divine names, *al-raḥmān* and *al-raḥīm* both of which are derived from the same root *raḥama*. Yet, these two names denote two different aspects of the Divine Mercy. *Al-raḥmān* is the transcendent aspect of Divine Mercy. It is a mercy which like the sky envelopes and contains all things. Were God to be without this all-encompassing mercy He would have never created the world. And it is through His mercy, through the 'Breath of the Compassionate' (*nafas al-raḥmān*), that He brought the world into being. That is why creation is good as also asserted in the Bible. The world of creation itself is not evil as was held by certain schools such as the Manichaeans. As for *al-raḥīm* it is the immanent mercy of God. It is like a ray of light which shines in our heart and touches individual lives and particular events. The two qualities combined express the totality of Divine Mercy which envelopes us from without and shines forth from within our being.

The *basmalah* opens every chapter of the Quran except one which is really the continuation of the previous chapter. It also opens the *Sūrat al-fātiḥah*, the opening chapter of the Quran, which is recited over and over again in the daily canonical prayers, and which contains the essence of the Quranic message. This chapter expresses the primordial relation between God and man. It consists of seven verses, three concerning God, three man, and one the relation between the two. In reciting its verses man stands in his primordial state before God, and prays in the name of all creatures and for all creatures. That is why its verbs are all in the first person plural and not the singular. It is the prayer of man as the conscious centre of all creation before the Creator and as such it contains symbolically the total message of the Quran.

The *basmalah* begins the *Sūrat al-fātiḥah* and therefore the whole of the Quran. It thus comes at the beginning of the prophetic message which is itself revealed because of God's mercy towards men. It is in reference to the inner meaning of this formula that 'Alī, the representative *par excellence* of esotericism in Islam, said that 'all the Quran is contained in the *Sūrat al-fātiḥah*, all of this *Sūrat* is contained in the *basmalah*, all of the *basmalah* in the letter *bā'* (ب) with which it begins, all of the letter *bā'* in the diacritical point under it and I am that diacritical point'.

The beautiful symbolism indicated in this saying refers to 'Alī's 'supreme identity' as the perfect saint who is inwardly in union with God. This point with which the *basmalah* begins is according to another *Ḥadīth* the first drop from the Divine Pen. It thus marks the beginning of things as it is also the beginning of the Quran. Like the point which generates all geometric space, this point is the symbol of the Origin of all creation, as the *basmalah* itself marks the beginning of things. Its recitation at the beginning of an act relates that act to God and sanctifies it. Even if every Muslim is not aware of all the metaphysical implications of the formula, yet its sanctifying power is known and felt by all and for that reason every act which is necessary and legitimate in life should begin with the *basmalah*, such as eating a meal or beginning a journey. In fact that act is illicit at whose commencement a devout Muslim cannot pronounce the formula. Otherwise all that is acceptable before the eyes of God can be sanctified by it. Through the *basmalah* the Divine joy and bliss enters into human life to bless and sanctify it.

Closely connected with the *basmalah* in meaning is the second *Shahādah*, *Muḥammadun rasūl Allāh*, Muḥammad is the Messenger of God, which again expresses the Divine mercy for the world, for the Prophet is mercy for this world and the next (*raḥmat Allāh li'l-'ālamīn*). He is the mercy of God for all worlds and through his aid man is able to lead a life of happiness here below and felicity in the world to come. The second *Shahādah* is the complement of the first. The first negates all otherness from God, the second asserts that all that is positive in creation, of which Muḥammad—Upon whom be peace—is the symbol, comes from God.

The *Alḥamduli'-llāh*, Praise be to God, which is so commonly used in everyday speech throughout the Muslim world, is the complement of the *basmalah*. It ends an act as the *basmalah* begins it. The *Alḥamd* integrates the positive content of every act into its Divine Origin and makes man conscious of the fact that whatever he has done that is good comes from God and returns to Him. This formula again cannot be iterated except after an act that is pleasing to God and that leaves a positive imprint upon the soul and again it is the criterion of the spiritual value of an act.

The formula, *Allāhu akbar* which is repeated during the call to prayer and also punctuates the different phases of the daily canonical prayers, is similar to the first *Shahādah* and is in a sense a commentary upon it. It means not only that 'God is great'; but being in the comparative and at the same time superlative form, which are not normally distinguished in Arabic, it implies that He is greater and also greatest. It means fundamentally that whatever one says of God He transcends it and is greater than it. It is thus a way of asserting the Infinite nature of God that transcends all limited descriptions and formulations of Him. In daily life the formula *Allāhu akbar* demonstrates also the insignificance of the human before the Divine, the weakness of the mightiest human power before the Divine Omnipotence and the awe which comes into being in the heart of a Muslim at the sight of wonders of creation and of human life that reveal this Omnipotence.

Finally, among the most common formulae used are the two *inshā'Allāh* and *māshā'Allāh*, 'if God Wills' and 'what God has willed', which are heard so often in daily speech. The first refers to the future and expresses man's confidence in God's Will and the realization that nothing can be achieved without His Will. This formula and the attitude that accompanies it, of course, apply to that aspect of reality which is connected with our free will, not that which follows from necessity. One does not say *inshā' Allāh*, three follows two or Monday comes after Sunday. One repeats this phrase about events in the future which despite all human effort cannot be realized with certainty except with Divine succour and consent. No matter how much we plan we do not know whether tomorrow we shall be here or elsewhere, or whether we shall be in the same state as now, and so we plan and act but fully conscious of the dependence of this action on the Divine Will, that Will which infinitely transcends ours. As for the *māshā' Allāh* it comes at the end of an act and again reminds us that, ultimately, whatever occurs comes from God, and that whatever is realized is not by human effort alone but through His Will.

There are of course other formulae, drawn mostly from the Quran and occasionally from the *Ḥadīth*, which is in reality a commentary upon the Sacred Text, from which the texture of the life of a Muslim is woven. These phrases are means by which God is remembered in daily life, in regular conversation and speech. Through these Quranic phrases the life of man, which is scattered in multiplicity, becomes integrated by a thread of 'remembrance' which runs through it. The very existence of these formulae in every day life is a reminder of the continual presence of the Quran and its message in Muslim life.

In summary, then, it can be said that the Quran is both a source of law to guide the practical life of man and of knowledge which inspires his intellectual endeavours. It is a universe into whose contours both the natural and social environment of man are cast, a universe which determines the life of the soul of man, its becoming, fruition, death and final destiny beyond this world. As such it is the central theophany of Islam, but one which would never have come to men and never been understood save for him who was chosen as its messenger and commentator to men. Once it was asked of the Prophet how he could be remembered and the nature of his soul known to the generations after him. He answered, 'By reading the Quran'. And it is in studying the life, teachings and significance of the Prophet that the full meaning of the message of Islam as contained in the Quran can be understood.

Suggestions for further reading

Arberry, A. J., *The Koran Interpreted*, 2 vols., London, Allen & Unwin, 1955. The most poetic translation of the Quran in English and one which conveys more than any other English translation some of the literary qualities of the original.

Corbin, H. (with the collaboration of S. H. Nasr and O. Yahya), *Histoire de la philosophie islamique*, Paris, Gallimard, 1964, Chapter I, 1. The first work in a European language by the most understanding and penetrating Western authority on Islamic philosophy which deals with Islamic intellectual life in all its richness and discusses the role of the Quran as the source and inspiration for Islamic philosophy.

—, 'L'Intériorisation du sens en herméneutique soufie iranienne,' *Eranos-Jahrbuch*, XXVI, Zurich, 1958. An excellent study of the Sufi method of interpreting the Quran.

Gibb, H. A. R., *Mohammadanism*, Chapter III. The most balanced and useful of the well-known introductions to Islam in English, especially in its treatment of the social and legal aspects of Islam and the role of the Quran in their formation.

—, *Studies on the Civilization of Islam*, Boston, Beacon Press, 1962, Chapter XI. Contains essays of much interest on the structure of religious thought in Islam, especially on the Quran and the Prophet.

Goldziher, I., *Die Richtungen der islamischen Koranauslegung*, Leiden, Neudruck, 1952. An analysis of the Quran which has much scientific value by one of the founders of Islamic studies in the West whose approach, however, is often in discord with the Islamic point of view especially concerning the *Ḥadīth* and Sufism.

Muhammad Ali, *The Holy Qur'ān*, Lahore, Ahmadiyyah Anjuman, 1951. An excellent English translation of the Quran made more useful by the fact that the translation appears side by side with the Arabic text. The notes are, however, written from the point of view of the Aḥmadīyah and do not always reflect the traditional Muslim understanding of the different verses of the Quran.

Pickthall, M. M., *The Meaning of the Glorious Koran*, New York, The New American Library, 1963. The standard translation of the Quran by an English Muslim that is valuable because of its exactness and conformity to the original.

Schuon, F., *Understanding Islam*, London, Allen & Unwin, 1963, Chapter II. An unrivalled analysis of the inner significance of the Quran for Muslims.

Stanton, H. U. W., *The Teaching of the Qur'ān*, London, Central Board of Missions, 1919. Although written by a missionary it contains a useful summary of the contents of the Quran and an index of its subject matter.

For additional suggestions see p. 178.

CHAPTER III

The Prophet and Prophetic Tradition The Last Prophet and Universal Man

The Prophet as the founder of Islam and the messenger of God's revelation to mankind is the interpreter *par excellence* of the Book of God; and his *Ḥadīth* and *Sunnah*, his sayings and actions, are after the Quran, the most important sources of the Islamic tradition. In order to understand the significance of the Prophet it is not sufficient to study, from the outside, historical texts pertaining to his life. One must view him also from within the Islamic point of view and try to discover the position he occupies in the religious consciousness of Muslims. When in any Islamic language one says *the* Prophet, it means Muḥammad—whose name as such is never iterated except that as a courtesy it be followed by the formula '*Ṣall'Allāhu 'alaihī wa sallam*', that is, 'may God's blessing and salutation be upon him'.

It is even legitimate to say that, in general, when one says *the* Prophet it means the prophet of Islam; for although in every religion the founder, who is an aspect of the Universal Intellect, becomes the Aspect, the Word, the Incarnation, nevertheless each founder emphasizes a certain aspect of the Truth and even typifies that aspect universally. Although there is belief in incarnation in many religions, when one says *the* Incarnation it refers to Christ who personifies this aspect. And although every prophet and saint has experienced 'enlightenment', *the* Enlightenment refers to the experience of the Buddha which is the most outstanding and universal embodiment of this experience. In the same manner the prophet of Islam is the prototype and perfect embodiment of prophecy and so in a profound sense is *the* Prophet. In fact in Islam every form of revelation is envisaged as a prophecy whose complete and total realization is to be seen in Muḥammad—Upon whom be peace. As the Sufi poet Maḥmūd Shabistarī writes in his incomparable *Gulshan-i rāz* (*The Secret Rose Garden*):

> The first appearance of prophethood was in Adam,
> And its perfection was in the 'Seal of the Prophets'.
> (Whinfield translation)
>
> نبوت راظهور از آدم آمد   کمالش در وجود خاتم آمد

It is difficult for a non-Muslim to understand the spiritual significance of the Prophet and his role as the prototype of the religious and spiritual life, especially if one comes from a Christian background. Compared to Christ, or to the Buddha for that matter, the earthly career of the Prophet seems often too human and too engrossed in the vicissitudes of social, economic and political activity to serve as a model for the spiritual life. That is why so many people who write today of the great spiritual guides of humanity are not able to understand and interpret him sympathetically. It is easier to see the spiritual radiance of Christ or even medieval saints, Christian or Muslim, than that of the Prophet, although the Prophet is the supreme saint in Islam without whom there would have been no sanctity whatsoever.

The reason for this difficulty is that the spiritual nature of the Prophet is veiled in his human one and his purely spiritual function is hidden in his duties as the guide of men and the leader of a community. It was the function of the Prophet to be, not only a spiritual guide, but also the organizer of a new social order with all that such a function implies. And it is precisely this aspect of his being that veils his purely spiritual dimension from foreign eyes. Outsiders have understood his political genius, his power of oratory, his great statesmanship, but few have understood how he could be the religious and spiritual guide of men and how his life could be emulated by those who aspire to sanctity. This is particularly true in the modern world in which religion is separated from other domains of life and most modern men can hardly imagine how a spiritual being could also be immersed in the most intense political and social activity.

Actually if the contour of the personality of the Prophet is to be understood he should not be compared to Christ or the

Buddha whose message was meant primarily for saintly men and who founded a community based on monastic life which later became the norm of a whole society. Rather, because of his dual function as 'king' and 'prophet', as the guide of men in this world and the hereafter, the Prophet should be compared to the prophet-kings of the Old Testament, to David and Solomon, and especially to Abraham himself. Or to cite once again an example outside the Abrahamic tradition, the spiritual type of the Prophet should be compared in Hinduism, to Rama and Krishna, who although in a completely different traditional climate, were *avātaras* and at the same time kings and householders who participated in social life with all that such activity implies as recorded in the *Mahabhārata* and the *Ramāyana*.

This type of figure who is at once a spiritual being and a leader of men has always been, relatively speaking, rare in the Christian West, especially in modern times. Political life has become so divorced from spiritual principles that to many people such a function itself appears as an impossibility in proof of which Westerners often point to the purely spiritual life of Christ who said, 'My Kingdom is not of this world.' And even historically the Occident has not witnessed many figures of this type unless one considers the Templars and in another context such devout kings as Charlemagne and St. Louis. The figure of the Prophet is thus difficult for many Occidentals to understand and this misconception to which often bad intention has been added is responsible for the nearly total ignorance of his spiritual nature in most works written about him in Western languages of which the number is legion. One could in fact say that of the major elements of Islam the real significance of the Prophet is the least understood to non-Muslims and especially to Occidentals.

The Prophet did participate in social life in its fullest sense. He married, had a household, was a father and moreover he was ruler and judge and had also to fight many wars in which he underwent painful ordeals. He had to undergo many hardships and experience all the difficulties which human life, especially that of the founder of a new state and society, implies. But within all these activities his heart rested in contentment with the Divine, and he continued inwardly to repose in the Divine Peace. In fact his participation in social and political life was precisely to integrate this domain into a spiritual centre.

The Prophet entertained no political or worldly ambition whatsoever. He was by nature a contemplative. Before being chosen as prophet he did not like to frequent social gatherings and activities. He led a caravan from Mecca to Syria passing through the majestic silence of the desert whose very 'infinity' induces man towards contemplation. He often spent long periods in the cave of Ḥirā' in solitude and meditation. He did not believe himself to be by nature a man of the world or one who was naturally inclined to seek political power among the Quraysh or social eminence in Meccan society although he came from the noblest family. It was in fact very painful and difficult for him to accept the burden of prophecy which implied the founding of not only a new religion but also a new social and political order. All the traditional sources, which alone matter in this case, testify to the great hardship the Prophet underwent by being chosen to participate in the active life in its most acute form. Modern studies on the life of the Prophet which depict him as a man who enjoyed fighting wars, are totally untrue and in fact a reversal of the real personality of the Prophet. Immediately after the reception of the first revelation the Prophet confessed to his wife, Khadījah, how difficult it was for him to accept the burden of prophecy and how fearful he was of all that such a mission implied.

Likewise, with the marriages of the Prophet, they are not at all signs of his lenience *vis-à-vis* the flesh. During the period of youth when the passions are most strong the Prophet lived with only one wife who was much older than he and also underwent long periods of abstinence. And as a prophet many of his marriages were political ones which, in the prevalent social structure of Arabia, guaranteed the consolidation of the newly founded Muslim community. Multiple marriage, for him, as is true of Islam in general, was not so much enjoyment as responsibility and a means of integration of the newly founded society. Besides, in Islam the whole problem of sexuality appears in a different light from that in Christianity and should not be judged by the same standards. The multiple marriages of the Prophet, far from pointing to his weakness towards 'the flesh', symbolize his patriarchal nature and his function, not as a saint who withdraws from the world, but as one who sanctifies the very life of the world by living in it and accepting it with the aim of integrating it into a higher order of reality.

The Prophet has also often been criticized by modern Western authors for being cruel and for having treated men harshly. Such a charge is again absurd because critics of this kind have forgotten that either a religion leaves the world aside, as Christ did, or integrates the world, in which case it must deal with such questions as war, retribution, justice, etc. When Charlemagne or some other Christian king thrust a sword into the breast of a heathen soldier he was, from the individual point of view, being cruel to that soldier. But on the universal plane this was a necessity for the preservation of a Christian civilization which had to defend its borders or perish. The same holds true for a Buddhist king or ruler, or for that matter any religious authority which seeks to integrate human society.

The Prophet exercised the utmost kindness possible and was harsh only with traitors. Now, a traitor against a newly founded religious community, which God has willed and whose existence is a mercy from heaven for mankind, is a traitor against the Truth itself. The harshness of the Prophet in such cases is an expression of Divine Justice. One cannot accuse God of being cruel because men die, or because there is illness and ugliness in the world. Every construction implies a previous destruction, a clearing of grounds for the appearance of a new form. This holds true not only in case of a physical structure but also in case of a new revelation which must clear the ground if it is to be a new social and political order as well as a purely religious one. What appears to some as the cruelty of the Prophet towards men is precisely this aspect of his function as the instrument of God for the establishment of a new world order whose homeland in Arabia was to be pure of any paganism and polytheism which if present would pollute the very source of this new fountain of life. As to what concerned his own person, the Prophet was always the epitome of kindness and generosity.

Nowhere is the nobility and generosity of the Prophet better exemplified than in his triumphant entry into Mecca, which in a sense highlights his earthly career. There, at a moment when the very people who had caused untold hardships and trials for the Prophet were completely subdued by him, instead of thinking of vengeance, which was certainly his due, he forgave them. One must study closely the almost unimaginable obstacles placed before the Prophet by these same people, of the immense suffering he had undergone because of them, to realize what degree of generosity this act of the Prophet implies. It is not actually necessary to give an apologetic account of the life of the Prophet, but these matters need to be answered because the false and often malicious accusations of this kind made against the founder of Islam in so many modern studies make the understanding of him by those who rely upon such studies well nigh impossible.

Also the Prophet was not certainly without love and compassion. Many incidents in his life and sayings recorded in *Ḥadīth* literature point to his depth of love for God which, in conformity with the general perspective of Islam, was never divorced from the knowledge of Him. For example, in a well known *Ḥadīth*, he said, 'O Lord, grant to me the love of thee. Grant that I love those that love thee. Grant that I may do the deed that wins thy love. Make thy love dear to me more than self, family and wealth.' Such sayings clearly demonstrate the fact that although the Prophet was in a sense a king or ruler of a community and a judge and had to deal according to justice in both capacities, he was at the same time one whose being was anchored in the love for God. Otherwise, he could not have been a prophet.

From the Muslim point of view, the Prophet is the symbol of perfection of both the human person and human society. He is the prototype of the human individual and the human collectivity. As such he bears certain characteristics in the eye of traditional Muslims which can only be discovered by studying the traditional accounts of him. The many Western works on the Prophet, with very few exceptions, are useless from this point of view no matter how much historical data they provide for the reader. The same holds true in fact for the new type of biographies of the Prophet written by modernized Muslims who would like at all cost to make the Prophet an ordinary man and neglect systematically any aspect of his being that does not conform to a humanistic and rationalistic framework they have adopted *a priori*, mostly as a result of either influence from or reaction to the modern Western point of view. The profound characteristics of the Prophet which have guided the Islamic community over the centuries and have left an indelible mark on the consciousness of the Muslim cannot be discerned save through the traditional sources and the *Ḥadīth*, and, of course, the Quran itself which bears the perfume of the soul of the person through whom it was revealed.

The universal characteristics of the Prophet are not the same as his daily actions and day to day life, which can be read about in standard biographies of the Prophet, and with which we cannot deal here. They are, rather; characteristics which issue forth from his personality as a particular spiritual prototype. Seen in this light there are essentially three qualities that characterize the Prophet. First of all the Prophet possessed the quality of piety in its most universal sense, that quality which attaches man to God. The Prophet was in that sense pious. He had a profound piety which inwardly attached him to God, that made him place the interest of God before everything else including himself. Secondly he had a quality of combativeness, of always being actively engaged in combat against all that negated the Truth and disrupted harmony. Externally it meant fighting wars, either military, political or social ones, the war which the Prophet named the 'little holy war' (*al-jihād al-aṣghar*). Inwardly this combativeness meant a continuous war against the carnal soul (*nafs*), against all that in man tends towards the negation of God and His Will, the 'great holy war' (*al-jihād al-akbar*).

It is difficult for modern men to understand the positive symbolism of war thanks to modern technology which has made war total and its instruments the very embodiment of what is ugly and evil. Men therefore think that the role of religion is only in preserving some kind of precarious peace. This, of course, is true, but not in the superficial sense that is usually meant. If religion is to be an integral part of life it must try to establish peace in the most profound sense, namely to establish equilibrium between all the existing forces that surround man and to overcome all the forces that tend to destroy this equilibrium. No religion has sought to establish peace in this sense more than Islam. It is precisely in such a context that war can have a positive meaning as the activity to establish harmony both inwardly and outwardly and it is in this sense that Islam has stressed the positive aspect of combativeness.

The Prophet embodies to an eminent degree this perfection of combative virtue. If one thinks of the Buddha as sitting in a state of contemplation under the Bo-tree, the Prophet can be imagined as a rider sitting on a steed with the sword of justice and discrimination drawn in his hand and galloping at full speed, yet ready to come to an immediate halt before the mountain of Truth. The Prophet was faced from the beginning of his prophetic mission with the task of wielding the sword of Truth, of establishing equilibrium and in this arduous task he had no rest. His rest and repose was in the heart of the holy war (*jihād*) itself and he represents this aspect of spirituality in which peace comes not in passivity but in true activity. Peace belongs to one who is inwardly at peace with the Will of Heaven and outwardly at war with the forces of disruption and disequilibrium.

Finally, the Prophet possessed the quality of magnanimity in its fullness. His soul displayed a grandeur which every devout Muslim feels. He is for the Muslim nobility and magnanimity personified. This aspect of the Prophet is fully displayed in his treatment of his companions which, in fact, has been the model for later ages and which all generations of Muslims have sought to emulate.

To put it another way, which focuses more sharply the personality of the Prophet, the qualities can be enumerated as strength, nobility and serenity or inner calm. Strength is outwardly manifested in the little holy war and inwardly in the great holy war according to the saying of the Prophet who, returning from one of the early wars, said, 'We have returned from the small *jihād* to the great *jihād*.' It is this great *jihād* which is of particular spiritual significance as a war against all those tendencies which pull the soul of man away from the Centre and Origin and bar him from the grace of heaven.

The nobility or generosity of the Prophet shows itself most of all in charity towards all men and more generally towards all beings. Of course this virtue is not central as in Christianity which can be called the religion of charity. But it is important on the human level and as it concerns the person of the Prophet. It points to the fact that there was no narrowness or pettiness in the soul of the Prophet, no limitation in giving of himself to others. A spiritual man is one who always gives to those around him and does not receive, according to the saying, 'It is more blessed to give than to receive.' It was characteristic of the Prophet to have always given till the last moment of his life. He never asked anything for himself and never sought to receive.

The aspect of serenity, which also characterizes all true expressions of Islam, is essentially the love of truth. It is to put the Truth before everything else. It is to be impartial, to be logical on the level of discourse, not to let one's emotions colour and prejudice one's intellectual judgment. It is not to be a rationalist, but to see the truth of things and to love the Truth above all else. To love the Truth is to love God who is the Truth, one of His Names being the Truth (*al-ḥaqq*).

If one were to compare these qualities of the Prophet, namely, strength, nobility and serenity, with those of the founders of the other great religions one would see that they are not necessarily the same because firstly, the Prophet was not himself the Divine Incarnation and secondly, because each religion emphasizes a certain aspect of the Truth. One cannot follow and emulate Christ in the same manner as the Prophet because in Christianity Christ is the God-man, the Divine Incarnation. One can be absorbed into his nature but he cannot be copied as the perfection of the human state. One can neither walk on water nor raise the dead to life. Still, when one thinks of Christianity and Christ another set of characteristics come to mind, such as divinity, incarnation, and on another level love, charity and sacrifice. Or when one thinks of the Buddha and Buddhism it is most of all the ideas of pity for the whole of creation, enlightenment and illumination and extinction in Nirvana that stand out.

In Islam, when one thinks of the Prophet who is to be emulated, it is the image of a strong personality that comes to mind, who is severe with himself and with the false and the unjust, and charitable towards the world that surrounds him. On the basis of these two virtues of strength and sobriety on the one hand and charity and generosity on the other, he is serene, extinguished in the Truth. He is that warrior on horseback who halts before the mountain of Truth, passive towards the Divine Will, active towards the world, hard and sober towards himself and kind and generous towards the creatures about him.

These qualities characteristic of the Prophet are contained

virtually in the sound of the second *Shahādah, Muḥammadun rasūl Allāh*, that is, Muḥammad is the Prophet of God, in its Arabic pronunciation, not in its translation into another language. Here again the symbolism is inextricably connected to the sounds and forms of the sacred language and cannot be translated. The very sound of the name Muḥammad implies force, a sudden breaking forth of a power which is from God and is not just human. The word *rasūl* with its elongated second syllable symbolizes this 'expansion of the chest' (*inshirāḥ al-ṣadr*), and a generosity that flows from the being of the Prophet and which ultimately comes from God. As for Allah it is, of course, the Truth itself which terminates the formula. The second *Shahādah* thus implies by its sound the power, generosity and serenity of reposing in the Truth characteristic of the Prophet. But this repose in the Truth is not based on a flight from the world but on a penetration into it in order to integrate and organize it. The spiritual castle in Islam is based on the firm foundations of harmony within human society and in individual human life.

In the traditional prayers on the Prophet which all Muslims recite on certain occasions, God's blessing and salutation are asked for the Prophet who is God's servant (*'abd*), His messenger (*rasūl*), and the unlettered Prophet (*al-nabī al-ummī*). For example, one well-known version of the formula of benediction upon the Prophet is as follows:

'Oh, God, bless our Lord Muḥammad, Thy servant and Thy Messenger, the unlettered Prophet, and his family and his companions, and salute them.'

(اللهم صل على سيدنا محمد عبدك ورسولك النبى الامى وعلى آله واصحابه وسلم)

Here again the three epithets with which his name is qualified symbolize his three basic characteristics which stand out most in the eyes of devout Muslims. He is first of all an *'abd*; but who is an *'abd* except one whose will is surrendered to the will of his master, who is himself poor (*faqīr*) but rich on account of what his master bestows upon him. As the *'abd* of God the Prophet exemplified in its fullness this spiritual poverty and sobriety which is so characteristic of Islam. He loved fasting, vigilance, prayer, all of which have become essential elements in Islamic religious life. As an *'abd* the Prophet put everything in the hands of God and realized a poverty which is, in reality, the most perfect and enduring wealth.

The *rasūl* in this formula again symbolizes his aspect of charity and generosity and metaphysically the *rasūl* himself is sent because of God's charity for the world and men whom He loves so that He sends His prophets to guide them. That is why the Prophet is 'God's mercy to the worlds.' For the Muslim the Prophet himself displays mercy and generosity, a generosity which flows from the nobility of character. Islam has always emphasized this quality and sought to inculcate nobility in the souls of men. A good Muslim must have some nobility and generosity which always reflect this aspect of the personality of the Prophet.

As for the *nabī al-ummī*, it symbolizes extinction before the Truth. The unlettered nature of the Prophet means most of all the extinction of all that is human before the Divine. The soul of the Prophet was a *tabula rasa* before the Divine Pen and on the human level his quality of 'unletteredness' marks that supreme virtue of realizing the Truth through the contemplation of it which marks an 'extinction' in the metaphysical sense before the Truth. Only through this extinction (*fanā'*) can one hope to enter into life with God and subsistence in Him (*baqā'*).

To summarize the qualities of the Prophet, it can be said that he is human equilibrium which has become extinct in the Divine Truth. He marks the establishment of harmony and equilibrium between all the tendencies present in man, his sensual, social, economic, political tendencies, which cannot be overcome unless the human state itself is transcended. He displays the integration of these tendencies and forces with the aim of establishing a basis which naturally leads towards contemplation and extinction in the Truth. His spiritual way means to accept the human condition which is normalized and sanctified as the ground for the most lofty spiritual castle. The spirituality of Islam of which the Prophet is the prototype is not the rejection of the world but the transcending of it through its integration into a Centre and the establishment of a harmony upon which the quest for the Absolute is based. The Prophet in these qualities that he displayed so eminently is at once the prototype of human and spiritual perfection and a guide towards its realization, for as the Quran states:

'Verily in the messenger of Allah ye have a good example.' (XXXIII, 21)

(لقدكان لكم فى رسول الله اسوة حسنة).

Since the Prophet is the prototype of all human perfection to the extent that one of his titles is the 'most noble of all creation' (*ashraf al-makhlūqāt*), it may be asked in what way can men emulate him. How can the Prophet become a guide for human life, and his life, deeds and thoughts serve as a guide for the Muslim in this terrestrial journey? The answer to this fundamental question, which concerns all the individual and collective life of Muslims of later generations, lies in the sayings which he left behind and which are known as *Ḥadīth* and his daily life and practice known as *Sunnah*. The family and companions of the Prophet who had been with him during his life time bore the impressions of his *Sunnah* within their souls with a depth that results from contact with a prophet. When man meets an extraordinary person he carries the impression of this meeting always. Then how permanent must have been the impression made on men by the Prophet, whose encounter is so much outside of ordinary experience today that human beings can hardly imagine it. The first generation of Muslims practiced this *Sunnah* with all the ardour and faith that resulted from their proximity to the source of the revelation and the presence of the *barakah* or grace of the Prophet among them. They in turn were emulated by the next generation and so on to modern times when the faithful still seek to base their lives upon that of the Prophet. This end is achieved through the fresh interpretation that each generation makes of his life (*siyar*), through the litanies and chants repeated in his praise (*madā'iḥ*) and through the celebrations marking his birth (*mawlid*) or other joyous occasions.

As for the *Ḥadīth*, these too were memorized by those who heard them and were in turn transmitted to those who followed during succeeding generations. Here again it was not a question of memorizing just anything but of remembering the sayings of one whom God had chosen as His messenger. And those who memorized the prophetic sayings were not like modern men whose memory has been dulled by formalized classroom learning and over-reliance on written sources, but nomads or men of nomadic background for whom speech and literature were connected with what was known by heart. These were men who possessed remarkable powers of memory, which still survive among certain so-called 'illiterate' people and which have often startled 'literate' observers from sedentary civilizations.

The sayings of the Prophet were eventually collected as the spread of Islam and the gradual moving away from the homogeneity of the early community endangered their integral existence. The devoutest of men set about to collect prophetic sayings or *Aḥādīth*, examining the chain of transmitters for each saying. As a result in the Sunni world six major collections of *Ḥadīth* became assembled such as those of Bukhārī and Muslim and soon gained complete authority in the orthodox community. In Shi'ism a similar process took place except that in addition to the sayings of the Prophet those of the Imams, whose teachings expound the meaning of the prophetic message, form a part of the *Ḥadīth* collection. There too, volumes of these sayings were assembled of which the most important is the *Uṣūl al-kāfī* of Kulainī.

The *Ḥadīth* literature, in both Sunni and Shi'ite sources, is a monumental treasury of wisdom which is at once a commentary upon the Quran and a complement to its teachings. The prophetic sayings concern every domain from pure metaphysics to table manners. In them one finds what the Prophet said at times of distress, in receiving an ambassador, in treating a prisoner, in dealing with his family, and in nearly every other situation which touches upon the domestic, economic, social and political life of man. In addition, in this literature many questions pertaining to metaphysics, cosmology, eschatology and the spiritual life are discussed. Altogether, after the Quran, the *Ḥadīth* and the prophetic *Sunnah* which is closely bound to it are the most precious source of guidance which Islamic society possesses, and along with the Quran they are the fountain head of all Islamic life and thought.

It is against this basic aspect of the whole structure of Islam that a severe attack has been made in recent years by an influential school of Western orientalists. No more of a vicious and insidious attack could be made against Islam than this one, which undercuts its very foundations and whose effect is more dangerous than if a physical attack were made against Islam.

Purporting to be scientific and applying the famous—or rather should one say the infamous—historical method which reduces all religious truths to historical facts, the critics of *Ḥadīth* have come to the conclusion that this literature is not from the Prophet but was 'forged' by later generations. What lies behind the scientific facade presented in most of these attacks is the *a priori* assumption that Islam is not a Divine revelation. If it is not a Divine revelation then it must be explained away in terms of factors present in seventh century Arabian society. Now, a Bedouin society could not have had any metaphysical knowledge, could not have possibly known about the Divine Word or Logos, about the higher states of being, about the structure of the Universe. Therefore, everything in *Ḥadīth* literature that speaks of these matters must be a later accretion. Were the critics of *Ḥadīth* simply to admit that the Prophet was a prophet, there would be no scientifically valid argument whatsoever against the main body of *Ḥadīth*. But this is precisely what they do not admit and therefore they have to consider as a later forgery anything in *Ḥadīth* literature which resembles the doctrines of other religions or speaks of esoteric questions.

There is of course no doubt that there are many *Ḥadīths* which are spurious. Traditional Islamic scholars themselves developed an elaborate science to examine the text of the *Ḥadīth* (*'ilm al-jarḥ*) and the validity of the chains of prophetic transmission (*'ilm al-dirāyah*) as well as the circumstances under which it was spoken. They sifted the sayings and compared them with detailed knowledge of the factors involved in a manner which no modern scholar can hope to match. In this manner certain sayings were accepted and other rejected as being either of dubious origin or completely unauthentic. Those who collected *Ḥadīth* were in fact the most pious and devout of men who often travelled from Central Asia to Medina or Iraq or Syria in search of *Ḥadīth*. Throughout Islamic history the most devout and ascetic of the religious scholars have been the scholars of *Ḥadīth*, (the *muḥaddithūn*), and because of the degree of piety and trust of the community that is necessary before a person is recognized as an authority in this field, they have always constituted the smallest number among all the different classes of religious scholars.

In fact what the modern critics of *Ḥadīth* do not realize in applying their so-called historical method is that they are projecting the kind of agnostic mentality prevalent in many academic circles today on to the mentality of a traditional Muslim scholar of *Ḥadīth*. They think that for him also the questions of religion could be treated in such a 'detached' manner as to enable them even to 'forge' sayings of the Prophet or to accept them into the traditional corpus without the greatest care. They do not realize that for men of the early centuries and especially the religious scholars the fire of hell was not an abstract thought but a concrete reality. They feared God in a way which most modern men can hardly imagine and it is psychologically absurd that, with a mentality to which the alternative of Heaven or Hell is the most real thing of all, they should commit the unpardonable sin of forging prophetic sayings. Nothing is less scientific than to project the modern mentality, which is an anomaly in history, on to a period when man lived and thought in a traditional world in which the verities of religion determined life itself, and in which men sought first and foremost to perform the most important duty placed upon their shoulders, namely, to save their souls.

As to the statement made by critics of *Ḥadīth* that the forged sayings came into being in the second century and were honestly believed to be prophetic sayings by the collectors of the third century, the same answer can be given. The *Sunnah* of the Prophet and his sayings had left such a profound imprint upon the first generation and those that came immediately afterwards that a forging of new sayings, and therefore also new ways of action and procedure in religious questions that already possessed precedence, would have been immediately opposed by the community. It would have meant a break in the continuity of the whole religious life and pattern of Islam which, in fact, is not discernible. Moreover, the Imams, whose sayings are included in the *Ḥadīth* corpus in Shi'ism and who themselves are the most reliable chain of transmission of prophetic sayings, survived after the third Islamic century, that is, after the very period of the collection of the well-known books of *Ḥadīth*, so that they bridge the period to which the modern critics point as the time of 'forgery' of *Ḥadīth*. Their very presence in fact is one more proof of the falsity of the arguments presented against the authenticity of *Ḥadīth* literature, arguments which attack not only the dubious and spurious sayings but the main body of *Ḥadīth*, according to which Islamic society has lived and modelled itself since its inception.

The danger inherent in this criticism of the *Ḥadīth* lies in decreasing its value in the eyes of those Muslims who, having come under the sway of its arguments, accept the fatally dangerous conclusion that the body of *Ḥadīth* is not the sayings of the Prophet and therefore does not carry his authority. In this way one of the foundations of Divine Law and a vital source of guidance for the spiritual life is destroyed. It is as if the whole foundation were pulled from underneath the structure of Islam. What would be left in such a case would be the Quran, which, being the Word of God, is too sublime to interpret and decipher without the aid of the Prophet. Left by themselves men would in most cases read their own limitations into the Holy Book and the whole homogeneity of Muslim society and the harmony existing between the Quran and the religious life of Islam would be disrupted. There are few problems that call for as immediate action on the part of the Muslim community as a response by qualified, traditional Muslim authorities in scientific—but not necessarily 'scientistic'—terms to the charges brought against *Ḥadīth* literature by modern Western critics, who have now also found a few disciples among Muslims. They have found a few followers of Muslim background who have left the traditional point of view and have become enamoured by the apparently scientific method of the critics which only hides an *a priori* presumption no Muslim can accept, namely the negation of the heavenly origin of the Quranic revelation and the actual prophetic power and function of the Prophet.

Be it as it may, as far as traditional Islam is concerned, which alone concerns us here, the *Ḥadīth* is, after the Quran, the most important source of both the Law, *Sharī'ah*, and the Spiritual way, *Ṭarīqah*. And it is the vital integrating factor in Muslim society, for the daily lives of millions of Muslims the world over have been modelled upon the prophetic *Sunnah* and *Ḥadīth*. For nearly fourteen hundred years Muslims have tried to awaken in the morning as the Prophet awakened, to eat as he ate, to wash as he washed himself, even to cut their nails as he did. There has been no greater force for the unification of the Muslim peoples than the presence of this common model for the minutest acts of daily life. A Chinese Muslim, although racially a Chinese, has a countenance, behaviour, manner of walking and acting that resembles in certain ways those of a Muslim on the coast of the Atlantic. That is because both have for centuries copied the same model. Something of the soul of the Prophet is to be seen in both places. It is this essential unifying factor, a common *Sunnah* or way of living as a model, that makes a bazaar in Morocco have a 'feeling' or *ambiance* of a bazaar in Persia, although the people in the two places speak a different language and dress differently. There is something in the air which an intelligent foreign observer will immediately detect as belonging to the same religious and spiritual climate. And this sameness is brought about firstly through the presence of the Quran and secondly, and in a more immediate and tangible way, through the 'presence' of the Prophet in his community by virtue of his *Ḥadīth* and *Sunnah.*

Through the *Ḥadīth* and *Sunnah* Muslims come to know both the Prophet and the message of the Quran. Without *Ḥadīth* much of the Quran would be a closed book. We are told in the Quran to pray but were it not for prophetic *Sunnah* we would not know how to pray. Something as fundamental as the daily prayers which are the central rite of Islam would be impossible to perform without the guidance of the prophetic practice. This applies to a thousand and one other situations so that it is almost unnecessary to emphasize the vital connection between the Quran and the practice and sayings of the Prophet whom God chose as its revealer and interpreter to mankind.

Before terminating this discussion about the *Ḥadīth* it should be pointed out that within the vast corpus of prophetic sayings there are forty which are called "sacred sayings' (*Ḥadīth qudsī*) which are not a part of the Quran but in which God speaks in the first person through the Prophet. These sayings although small in number are of extreme importance in that they are, along with certain verses of the Quran, the basis of the spiritual life in Islam. Sufism is based on these sayings and many a Sufi knows them by heart and lives in constant remembrance of their message. These sayings all concern the spiritual life rather than social or political matters. They deal with man's direct relation with God as in the famous *Ḥadīth qudsī* so often repeated by Sufi masters over the ages: 'My slave ceaseth not to draw nigh unto Me through devotions of free-will until I love him, and when I love him, I am the hearing with which he heareth and the sight with which he seeth and the hand with which he fighteth and the foot with which he walketh.'

The presence of these sayings indicate how deeply the roots of Islamic spirituality are sunk in the sources of the revelation itself. Far from being just a legal and social system devoid of a spiritual dimension, or one upon which a spiritual dimension was artificially grafted later on, Islam was, from the beginning, both a Law and a Way. The two dimensions of Islam, the exoteric and esoteric, are best demonstrated in the case of the Prophet himself who was both the perfection of human action on the social and political plane and the prototype of the spiritual life in his inner oneness with God and in his total realization in which he saw nothing except in God and through God.

The particularity of the Prophet which distinguishes him from those that came before him is that he is the last of the prophets (*khātam al-anbiyā'*), the seal of prophecy who, coming at the end of the prophetic cycle, integrates in himself the function of prophecy as such. This aspect of the Prophet immediately brings up the question of what prophecy itself means. There have been numerous volumes written by traditional Muslim authorities on this subject in which the elaborate metaphysical dimension of this central reality of religion is outlined. Although it is not possible to discuss this question in detail here one can summarize by saying that prophethood is, according to the Islamic view, a state bestowed upon men whom God has chosen because of certain perfections in them by virtue of which they become the instrument through whom God reveals His message to the world. Their inspiration is directly from Heaven. A prophet owes nothing to anyone. He is not a scholar who discerns through books certain truths, nor one who learns from other human beings and in turn transmits this learning. His knowledge marks a direct intervention of the Divine in the human order, an intervention which is not, from the Islamic point of view, an incarnation but a theophany (*tajallī*).

This definition of prophethood holds true for every prophet, not just in the case of the founder of Islam. From the Muslim point of view Christ did not gain his knowledge of the Old

Testament and the message of the Hebrew prophets by reading books or learning from rabbis but directly from heaven. Nor did Moses learn the laws and the message that he brought from older prophets, be it even Abraham. He received a new message directly from God. And if he reiterated some of the truths of the messages brought by the Semitic prophets before him or if Christ affirmed the Jewish tradition whose inner meaning he revealed—according to the well-known saying 'Christ revealed what Moses veiled'—or if the Quran mentions some of the stories of the Old and New Testaments, none of these instances implies an historical borrowing. They indicate only a new revelation in the cadre of the same spiritual climate which can be called the Abrahamic tradition. The same applies to the *avātaras* of Hinduism who came each with a new message from Heaven but spoken in the language of the same spiritual ambiance.

Although all prophecy implies a meeting of the Divine and human planes, there are degrees of prophecy dependent upon the type of message revealed and the function of the messenger in propagating that message. In fact whereas in English the single word prophet is usually used, in Arabic, Persian and other languages of the Islamic people there are a series of words connected with levels of prophethood. There is first of all the *nabī*, a man who brings news of God's message, a man whom God has chosen to speak to. But God does not just speak to any man. He who is worthy of hearing a Divine message must be qualified. He must be pure by nature. That is why according to traditional Islamic sources the body of the Prophet was made from the choicest earth. He must possess the perfection of human virtues such as goodness and nobility although in reality he has nothing of his own, everything having been given by God to him. He must have the perfection of both the practical and theoretical faculties, a perfect imagination, an intellect that is perfectly attuned to the Divine Intellect, a psychological and corporeal structure which enables him to lead men in action and to guide them through all trials and circumstances. But the message which the *nabī* receives is not necessarily universal. He may receive a message which is to remain within him and not be divulged openly or is meant to be imparted to only a few in the cadre of an already existing religion.

Of the prophets in this sense (*anbiyā'*), there are, according to tradition, one-hundred and twenty-four thousand whom God has sent to every nation and people, for the Quran asserts that there is no people unto whom a prophet has not been sent. 'And for every nation there is a messenger' (X, 48),

(ولكل امة رسول)

although it also states that to each people God speaks in its own language, hence the diversity of religions. 'And We never sent a messenger save with the language of his folk' (XIV, 4)

(وما ارسلنا من رسول الا بلسان قومه)

The universality of prophecy so clearly enunciated in the Quran means the universality of tradition, of religion. It means that all orthodox religions come from heaven and are not man made. It also implies by its comprehensive formulation the presence of Divine revelation not only in the Abrahamic tradition but among all nations, although in previous times this question was not explored explicitly. The Quran asserted the principle of universality leaving the possibility of its application outside the Semitic world as the case arose, for example, when Islam encountered Zoroastrianism in Persia or Hinduism in India. In the same manner it could be applied in modern times to the encounter with any previously unknown genuine tradition, be it that of the American Indians.

Among the *anbiyā'* there are those who belong to another category of prophets, or a new level of prophecy, namely those who not only receive a message from heaven but are also chosen to propagate that message for the segment of humanity providentially destined for it. The prophet with such a function is called *rasūl*. He is also a *nabī* but in addition he has this function of making God's message known to men and inviting them to accept it, as is seen in the case of many prophets of the Old Testament. Above the *rasūl* stands the prophet who is to bring a major new religion to the world, the 'possessor of firmness and determination' (*ūlu'l-'azm*). Of this latter category Islam, again limiting itself to the Abrahamic Tradition, believes there have been seven, each of whom was the founder of a new religion and who brought a new Divine Law into the world. There are then altogether three grades of prophecy, that of the *nabī*, the *rasūl* and the *ūlu'l-'azm*, although in certain Islamic sources this gradation is further refined to include in further detail the degrees of *anbiyā'* who are distinguished by the manner in which they perceive the angel of revelation.

'The Prophet' was at once a *nabī*, a *rasūl* and an *ūlu'l-'azm* and brought the cycle of prophecy to a close. After him there will be no new *Sharī'ah* or Divine Law brought into the world until the end of time. There are to be no revelations (*waḥy*) after him, for he marks the termination of the prophetic cycle (*dā'irat al-nubuwwah*). It may on the surface appear as a great tragedy that man seems to be thus left without any possibility of renewing the truths of the revelation through new contact with the source of the truth. But in reality the termination of the prophetic cycle does not mean that all possibility of contact with the Divine order has ceased. Whereas revelation (*waḥy*) is no longer possible, inspiration (*ilhām*) remains always as a latent possibility. Whereas the cycle of prophecy (*dā'irat al-nubuwwah*) has come to an end, the cycle of *wilāyat* (*dā'irat al-wilāyah*), which for want of a better term may be translated as the 'cycle of initiation' and also sanctity, continues.

Actually *wilāyah* in this context, which should in the technical language of Islamic gnosis be distinguished from *wilāyah* in the ordinary sense having to do with the state of *walī* or saint, means the presence of this inner dimension within Islam which the Prophet inaugurated along with a new *Sharī'ah* and which will continue to the end of time. Thanks to its presence, man is able to renew himself spiritually and gain contact with the Divine although a new revelation is no longer possible. It is due to this esoteric dimension of Islam and the grace or *barakah* contained in the organizations which are its preservers and propagators that the spiritual force of the original revelation has been renewed over the ages and the possibility of a spiritual life leading to the state of sainthood, that purifies human society and rejuvenates religious forces, has been preserved.

The Prophet in terminating the prophetic cycle and in bringing the last *Sharī'ah* into the world, also inaugurated the cycle of 'Muhammadan sanctity' (*wilāyah muḥammadīyah*), which is ever present and which is the means whereby the spiritual energy of the tradition is continuously renewed. Therefore, far from there being a need for any new religion, which at this moment of time can only mean a pseudo-religion, the revelation brought by the Prophet contains in itself all that is needed to fulfil in every way the religious and spiritual needs of Muslims, from the common believer to the potential saint.

The Prophet, besides being the leader of men and the founder of a new civilization, is also the perfection of the human norm and the model for the spiritual life of Islam. He said 'I am a human being like you' (*anā basharun mithlukum*), to which Muslim sages over the ages have added, yes, but like a precious gem among stones (*ka'l-yāqūt bain al-ḥajar*). The profound symbolism contained in this saying is connected with the inner nature of the Prophet. All men in their purely human nature are like stones, opaque and heavy and a veil to the light that shines upon them. The Prophet also possesses this human nature outwardly. But inwardly he has become alchemically transmuted into a precious stone which, although still a stone, is transparent before the light and has lost its opacity. The Prophet is outwardly only a human being (*bashar*), but inwardly he is the full realization of manhood in its most universal sense. He is the Universal Man (*al-insān al-kāmil*), the prototype of all of creation, the norm of all perfection, the first of all beings, the mirror in which God contemplates universal existence. He is inwardly identified with the Logos and the Divine Intellect.

In every religion the founder is identified with the Logos, as we read in the beginning of the Gospel according to John, '*In principio erat verbum*', that is, that which was in the beginning was the Word or Logos identified with Christ. Islam considers all prophets as an aspect of the Universal Logos, which in its perspective is identified with the 'Reality of Muḥammad' (*al-ḥaqīqat al-muḥammadīyah*), which was the first of God's creation and through whom God sees all things. As the Muḥammadan reality the Prophet came before all the other prophets at the beginning of the prophetic cycle, and it is to this inner aspect of him as the Logos to which reference is made in the *Ḥadīth* 'He [Muḥammad] was prophet [the Logos] when Adam was still between water and clay.'

(فكان نبياً وآدم بين الماء والطين)

The Sufi Najm al-Dīn al-Rāzī in his *Mirṣād al-'ibād* writes that just as in the case of a tree one first plants a seed which then grows into a plant that gives branches, then leaves, then blossoms, then fruit which in turn contains the seed, so did the cycle of prophecy begin with the Muḥammadan Reality, with the inner reality of Muḥammad, while it ended with the human manifestation of him. He thus is inwardly the beginning and outwardly the end of the prophetic cycle which he synthesizes and unifies in his being. Outwardly he is a human being and inwardly the Universal Man, the norm of all spiritual perfection. The Prophet himself referred to this inner aspect of his nature as in the *Ḥadīth*, 'I am Aḥmad without the *mīm* [that is, *aḥad* meaning Unity]; I am an Arab without the (*'ain*) [that is *rabb* meaning Lord]. Who hath seen me, the same hath seen the Truth.'

(انا احمد بلاميم، انا عربی بلاعین، من رآنی فقد رای الحق)

What do such sayings mean but the inward union of the Prophet with God. This truth has been re-iterated over and over again throughout the ages by masters of Sufism as in the beautiful Persian poem from the *Gulshan-i rāz*:

A single *mim* divides Aḥad from Aḥmad
The world is immersed in that one *mim*.

(زاحمد تا احد یك میم فرق است　　　جهانی اندر این یك میم غرق است)

This '*mim*' which separates the esoteric name of the Prophet, Aḥmad, from God, is the symbol of return to the Origin, of death and reawakening to the eternal realities. Its numerical equivalence is forty which itself symbolizes the age of prophecy in Islam. The Prophet is outwardly the messenger of God to men; inwardly he is in permanent union with the Lord.

The doctrine of Universal Man which is inextricably connected with what one may call prophetology in Islam, is far from having originated as a result of later influences upon Islam. It is based rather on what the Prophet was inwardly and as he was seen by those among his companions who, besides being his followers religiously, were the inheritors of his esoteric message. Those who wish to deprive Islam of a spiritual and intellectual dimension seek to make of this basic doctrine a later borrowing as if the Prophet could have become in an effective and operative way the Universal Man by just having such a state attributed to him if he were not so already in his real nature. It would be as if one expected a body to shine simply by calling it the sun. The Prophet possessed in himself that reality which later gained the technical name of Universal Man. But the 'named' was there long before this name was given to it, and before the theory of it was elaborated for later generations who because of elongation from the source of the revelation were in need of further explanation.

In conclusion it may be said that the Prophet is the perfection of both the human collectivity and the human individual, the norm for the perfect social life and the prototype and guide for the spiritual life. He is both the Universal Man and the Primordial Man (*al-insān al-qadīm*). As the Universal Man he is the totality of which we are a part and in which we participate; as the Primordial Man he is that original perfection with respect to which we are a decadence and a falling away. He is thus both the 'spatial' and 'temporal' norms of perfection, 'spatial' in the sense of the totality of which we are a part and 'temporal' in the sense of the perfection which was at the beginning and which we must seek to regain by moving upstream against the downward flow of the march of time.

The Prophet possessed eminently both the human (*nāsūt*) and spiritual (*lāhūt*) natures. Yet, there was never an incarnation of the *lāhūt* into the *nāsūt*, a perspective which Islam does not accept. The Prophet did possess these two natures and for this very reason his example makes possible the presence of a spiritual way in Islam. He was the perfect ruler, judge and leader of men. He was the creator of the most perfect Muslim society in comparison with which every later society is a falling away. But he was in addition the prototype of the spiritual life. That is why it is absolutely necessary to follow in his footsteps if one aspires towards spiritual realization.

The love of the Prophet is incumbent upon all Muslims and especially upon those who aspire towards the saintly life. This love must not be understood in an individualistic sense. Rather, the Prophet is loved because he symbolizes that harmony and beauty that pervade all things, and displays in their fullness those virtues, the attainment of which allow man to realize his theomorphic nature.

'Lo! Allah and His angels shower blessings on the Prophet.
O ye who believe!
Ask blessings on him and salute him with a worthy salutation.'
(XXXIII, 56)

(ان الله وملائكته يصلون عل النبى ياايها الذين آمنوا صلوا عليه وسلموا تسليما)

Suggestions for further reading

Dermenghem, E., *The Life of Mahomet*, London, Routledge, 1930. A well written and revealing account of the life of the Prophet which describes especially the significance of the various events of his life.

Dinet, E. and El Hadj Sliman Ben Ibrahim, *La Vie de Mohammed, Prophète d'Allah*, Paris, G.-P. Maisonneuve, 1947. A thorough, traditional account of the Prophet's life.

Essad Bey, M., *Mahomet*, Paris, Payot, 1934. The life of the Prophet by a European convert to Islam.

Gheorghiu, G., *La Vie de Mahomet*, Paris, Gallimard, 1964. The most moving and poetic account of the life of the Prophet by a leading European novelist and poet showing much sympathy and understanding.

Goldsack, W., *Selections from Muhammadan Traditions*, Madras, Christian Literature Society, 1923. A translation of a selection of one of the well-known traditional collections of *Ḥadīth*.

Guillaume, A. (trans.), *The Life of Muhammad, a translation of Ishāq's Sīrat Rasūl Allāh*, London, Oxford University Press, 1955. The English translation of the *Sīrah* of Ibn Isḥāq, the most important traditional Muslim source on the life of the Prophet.

Hamidullah, M., *Le Prophète de l'Islam*, 2 vols., Paris, J. Vin, 1959. A detailed historical account of the background and life of the Prophet by a modern Muslim scholar.

Guénon, R., *Symbolism of the Cross*, trans. by A. Macnab, London, Luzac, 1958. A profound analysis of the idea of universal man and its role in Islamic esotericism.

Ikbal Ali Shah, Sirdar, *Mohamed: the Prophet*, London, Wright & Brown, 1932. A readable account of the Prophet's life and times by a modern Muslim author.

al-Jīlī, 'Abd al-Karīm, *De l'Homme universel*, trans. by T. Burckhardt, Lyon, P. Derain, 1953. A masterly translation and analysis of the classical Sufi work on Universal Man.

Muhammad Ali, *A Manual of Hadith*, Lahore, Ahmadiyya Anjuman, 1951. A translation of some of the prophetic sayings covering different subjects and giving a good selection of *Ḥadīth* literature.

Rahnema, Z., *Le Prophète*, Paris, La Colombe, 1957. The French version of a modern biography of the Prophet which has been read more than any other work of its kind in Persian and combines historical reporting with poetical treatment.

Rauf, M. A., *The Life and Teaching of the Prophet Muḥammad*, London, Longmans, 1964. A brief but useful traditional introduction to the life of the Prophet by a modern Muslim.

Schuon, F., *Understanding Islam*, London, Allen & Unwin, 1965, Chapter III. The best account in European languages on the spiritual significance of the Prophet.

Suhrawardy, A., *The Sayings of Muhammad*, London, J. Murray, 1941. An excellent selection of *Ḥadīth* literature which despite its shortness displays the grandeur and beauty of prophetic utterances.

al-Tabrīzī, *Mishkāt al-maṣābīḥ*, English translation with explanatory notes by J. Robson, 4 vols., Lahore, Muhammad Ashraf, 1963–65. Perhaps the most valuable translation of *Ḥadīth* in English containing some 5950 different traditions assembled from major Sunni canonical collections.

Watt, G. M., *Muhammad, Prophet and Statesman*, London, Oxford University Press, 1961. A study of the career of the Prophet which is of value for its analysis of the social forces present and is more sympathetic than most Western works on the subject.

Yusuf, S. M., *An Essay on the Sunnah*, Karachi, Institute of Islamic Culture, 1966. An orthodox study and defense of the origin and significance of the prophetic Sunnah.

CHAPTER IV

The Sharī'ah
Divine Law—Social and Human Norm

The *Sharī'ah* is the Divine Law by virtue of accepting which a person becomes a Muslim. Only he who accepts the injunctions of the *Sharī'ah* as binding upon him is a Muslim although he may not be able to realize all of its teachings or follow all of its commands in life. The *Sharī'ah* is the ideal pattern for the individual's life and the Law which binds the Muslim people into a single community. It is the embodiment of the Divine Will in terms of specific teachings whose acceptance and application guarantees man a harmonious life in this world and felicity in the hereafter.

The word *Sharī'ah* itself is derived etymologically from a root meaning road. It is the road which leads to God. It is of great symbolic significance that both the Divine Law and the Spiritual Way or *Ṭarīqah*, which is the esoteric dimension of Islam, are based on the symbolism of the way or journey. All life is a sojourn, a journey through this transient world to the Divine Presence. The *Sharī'ah* is the wider road which is meant for all men by virtue of which they are able to attain the total possibilities of the individual human state. The *Ṭarīqah* is the narrower path for the few who have the capability and profound urge to attain sanctity here and now and seek a path whose end is the full realization of the reality of Universal Man transcending the individual domain.

The *Sharī'ah* is Divine Law, in the sense that it is the concrete embodiment of the Divine Will according to which man should live in both his private and social life. In every religion the Divine Will manifests itself in one way or another and the moral and spiritual injunctions of each religion are of Divine origin. But in Islam the embodiment of the Divine Will is not a set only of general teachings but of concrete ones. Not only is man told to be charitable, humble or just, but how to be so in particular instances of life. The *Sharī'ah* contains the injunctions of the Divine Will as applied to every situation in life. It is the Law according to which God wants a Muslim to live. It is therefore the guide of human action and encompasses every facet of human life. By living according to the *Sharī'ah* man places his whole existence in God's 'hand'. The *Sharī'ah* by considering every aspect of human action thus sanctifies the whole of life and gives a religious significance to what may appear as the most mundane of activities.

The lack of understanding of the significance of the *Sharī'ah* in the Western world is due to its concrete and all-embracing nature. A Jew who believes in Talmudic Law can understand what it means to have a Divine Law whereas for most Christians, and therefore for secularists with a Christian background, such an understanding comes with difficulty, precisely because in Christianity there is no clear distinction between the law and the way. In Christianity the Divine Will is expressed in terms of universal teachings such as being charitable, but not in concrete laws.

The difference between the conception of Divine Law in Islam and in Christianity can be seen in the way the word canon (*qānūn*) is used in the two traditions. This word was borrowed in both cases from the Greek. In Islam it has come to denote a man-made law in contrast to the *Sharī'ah* or divinely inspired Law. In the West the opposing meaning is given to this word in the sense that canonical law refers to laws governing the ecclesiastical organization of the Catholic and Episcopal churches, and has a definitely religious colour.

The Christian view concerning law which governs man socially and politically is indicated in the well-known saying of Christ, 'Render therefore unto Caesar the things which are Caesar's'. This phrase has actually two meanings of which only one is usually considered. It is commonly interpreted as leaving all things that are worldly and have to do with political and social regulations to secular authorities of whom Caesar is the outstanding example. But more than that it also means that because Christianity, being a spiritual way, had no Divine legislation of its own, it had to absorb Roman Law in order to become the religion of a civilization. The law of Caesar, or the Roman Law, became providentially absorbed into the Christian perspective once this religion became dominant in the West, and it is to this fact that the saying of Christ alludes. The dichotomy, however, always remained. In Christian civilization law governing human society did not enjoy the same Divine sanction as the teachings of Christ. In fact this lack of a Divine Law in Christianity had no small role to play in the secularization that took place in the West during the Renaissance. It is also the most important cause for the lack of understanding of the meaning and role of the *Sharī'ah* on the part of Westerners as well as so many modernized Muslims.

With regard to the Divine Law, however, the situation of Islam and Christianity differ completely. Islam never gave unto Caesar what was Caesar's. Rather, it tried to integrate the domain of Caesar itself, namely, political, social and economic life, into an encompassing religious world view. Law is therefore in Islam an integral aspect of the revelation and not an alien element. Of course Roman Law also possessed a religious colour in the Roman religion itself, and the function of 'The Divine Caesar' was to establish order on earth, through this law. But from the point of view of Christianity it was a foreign component without the sanctifying authority of revelation. In the Christian West law was thus from the beginning something human to be made and revised according to the needs and circumstances of the times. The Western attitude towards law is totally determined by the character of Christianity as a spiritual way which did not bring a revealed law of its own.

The Semitic notion of law which is universalized in both Judaism and Islam is the opposite of the prevalent Western conception of law. It is a religious notion of law, one in which law is an integral aspect of religion. In fact religion to a Muslim *is* essentially the Divine Law which includes not only universal moral principles but details of how man should conduct his life and deal with his neighbour and with God; how he should eat, procreate and sleep; how he should buy and sell at the market place; how he should pray and perform other acts of worship. It includes all aspect of human life and contains in its tenets the guide for a Muslim to conduct his life in harmony with the Divine Will. It guides man towards an understanding of the Divine Will by indicating which acts and objects are from the religious point of view obligatory (*wājib*), which are meritorious or recommended (*mandūb*), which are forbidden (*ḥarām*), which reprehensible (*makrūh*), and which indifferent (*mubāḥ*). Through this balance the value of human acts in the sight of the Divine are made known to man so that he can distinguish between the 'Straight Path' and that which will lead him astray. The *Sharī'ah* provides for him the knowledge of right and wrong. It is by his free will that man must choose which path to follow.

Such a Law is the blue print of the ideal human life. It is a transcendent law which is at the same time applied in human society, but never fully realized because of the imperfections of all that is human. The *Sharī'ah* corresponds to a reality that transcends time and history. Rather, each generation in Muslim society should seek to conform to its teachings and apply it anew to the conditions in which it finds itself. The creative process in each generation is not to remake the Law but to reform men and human society to conform to the law. According to the Islamic view religion should not be reformed to conform to the ever changing and imperfect nature of men but men should reform so as to live according to the tenets of revelation. In accordance with the real nature of things it is the human that must conform to the Divine and not the Divine to the human.

The movement of reform throughout Islamic history has been to seek to recreate and reshape human attitudes and social institutions so as to make them harmonious with the *Sharī'ah*. It has been to revivify and revitalize human society by continuously infusing its structure with the principles of the revelation which are providentially sent as its guide and which alone provide a criterion for its own worth and value. Those modern movements which seek to reform the Divine Law rather than human society are, from the Islamic point of view, in every way an anomaly. Such movements are brought about to a great extent not only through the weakening of religious faith among certain men but also because the modern mentality, which originated in the West with its Christian background, cannot conceive of an immutable Law which is the guide of human society and upon which man should seek to model his individual and social life. There is no better proof of how deeply rooted man's religious heritage is than the modern Western attitude towards law which is the same as that of Christianity although so many who have created and who uphold the modern view do not consider themselves as Christians and some even are opposed to Christianity.

The *Sharī'ah* is for Islam the means of integrating human society. It is the way by which man is able to give religious significance to his daily life and be able to integrate this life into a spiritual centre. Man lives in multiplicity; he lives and acts according to multiple tendencies within himself, some of which issue from animal desires, others from sentimental or rational or yet spiritual aspects of his being. Man faces this multiplicity within himself and at the same time lives in a society of which he is a part and with whose members he has an indefinite number of contacts and relations. All of these activities, these norms of doing and existing in the human condition, cannot be integrated and cannot find meaning save in the *Sharī'ah*. The Divine Law is like a network of injunctions and attitudes which govern all of human life and in their totality and all-embracing nature are able to integrate man and society according to the dominating principle of Islam itself, namely unity or *tawḥīd*. The *Sharī'ah* is the means by which unity is realized in human life.

Seen from the outside, this role of the *Sharī'ah* may be difficult to understand. On the surface it seems to contain laws about how to marry, trade, divide inheritance or conduct the affairs of state. These are all acts performed in the world of time and multiplicity. How can they then be integrated so as to reflect unity? The answer is that these actions are still actions whether they are performed according to the *Sharī'ah* or not. But the effect that such actions leave on the souls of men is completely different depending on whether the act is performed simply according to man-made laws or whether it follows the teachings of the *Sharī'ah*. In the latter case the religious context in which the act is placed and the inner connection that the teachings of the *Sharī'ah* have to the spiritual life of man transform an otherwise secular act into a religious one. Instead of the soul scattering itself over countless forms of action, the action itself leaves a positive imprint upon the soul and aids towards its integration.

There is a *Ḥadīth* according to which when a man works to feed his family he is performing as much an act of worship as if he were praying. This statement may be difficult to understand by one not acquainted with the traditional way of life. In modern society it is not possible to find religious significance in most actions and except for a few offices directly connected with the administration of religious needs, most professions through which men gain their livelihood are devoid of a direct religious significance. The breaking up of traditional Christian society, in which every act was endowed with a religious significance, long ago secularized a large domain of human life in the West. A contemporary who wishes to integrate all of his life finds great difficulty in giving religious significance to the daily work which he must of necessity perform.

The *Sharī'ah* makes the act of earning one's daily bread a religious act, one which a Muslim should perform with the awareness that he is performing an act that is pleasing in the sight of God and is as obligatory as specifically religious duties. The *Sharī'ah* in fact gives a religious connotation to all the acts that are necessary to human life, and of course not those which are simple luxuries. In this way the whole of man's life and activities become religiously meaningful. Were it to be otherwise man would be a house divided unto itself, in a condition of inner division and separation which Islam tries to avoid. Man by placing his life in the channels ordained by the *Sharī'ah* avoids many unseen catastrophes and assures himself a life of wholeness and meaning.

Some may object that accepting the *Sharī'ah* totally destroys human initiative. Such a criticism, however, fails to understand the inner workings of the Divine Law. The Law places before men many paths according to his nature and needs within a universal pattern which pertains to everyone. Human initiative comes in selecting what is in conformity with one's needs and living according to the Divine norm as indicated by the *Sharī'ah*. Initiative does not come only in rebelling against the Truth which is an easy task since stones fall by nature; initiative and creativity come most of all in seeking to live in conformity with the Truth and in applying its principles to the conditions which destiny has placed before man. To integrate all of one's tendencies and activities within a divinely ordained pattern requires all the initiative and creative energy which man is capable of giving.

To the Muslim the *Sharīʿah* is an eternal and transcendent law and the question of how it became codified and systematized in detail has not been of much interest until modern times. The studies of orientalists, which are usually historical, have directed attention to the gradual process by which the *Sharīʿah* became codified into the form in which the Islamic world has known it for the past millennium. It is therefore not without interest for us to consider how this process took place, although it must be made clear that the fact that the Divine Law was explicitly formulated in its final form after several stages does not in any way diminish from its Divine nature and the immutability of its injunctions.

In essence all of the *Sharīʿah* is contained in the Quran. The Holy Book, however, contains the principle of all the Law. It contains the Law potentially but not actually and explicitly, at least not all the different aspects of the *Sharīʿah*. There was therefore, a gradual process by which this Law became promulgated in its external form and made applicable to all domains of human life. This process was completed in about three centuries during which the great books of law in both Sunni and Shiʿite Islam were written, although the exact process is somewhat different in the two cases.

The principles of the Law contained in the Quran were explained and amplified in the prophetic *Ḥadīth* and *Sunnah,* which together constitute the second basic source of Law. These in turn were understood with the aid of the consensus of the Islamic community (*ijmāʿ*). Finally, these sources of Law were complemented by analogical human reasoning (*qiyās*) where necessary. According to the traditional Islamic view therefore, the sources of the *Sharīʿah* are the Quran, *Ḥadīth*, *ijmāʿ* and *qiyās* of which the first two are the most important and are accepted by all schools of law while the other two are either considered of lesser importance or rejected by some of the schools.

The meaning of the Quran and *Ḥadīth* is clear enough, but a few words must be said about the other two sources. As far as *ijmāʿ* is concerned it means the consensus of the Islamic community on some point of the Law and is considered important on the authority of the *Ḥadīth*: 'My community shall never agree in error'. Some modernized Muslims, who instead of wanting to make man God-like wish to make God man-like, especially like Twentieth century man, have tried simply to equate *ijmā'* with parliamentary 'democracy'. This, however, is not exactly the case because first of all *ijmā'* can operate only where the Quran and *Ḥadīth* have not clarified a certain aspect of the Law, so that its function is in this sense limited, and secondly it is a gradual process through which the community over a period of time comes to give its consensus over a question of Law. Finally, the view of Muslims over the centuries has been that giving opinion on problems of Law should be the function of the *'ulamā'*, who alone are well-versed in the science of Law. The sciences connected with the *Sharī'ah* are complex and require study before one can claim to be an authority in them. One could do no more than ask the consensus of a body of laymen on the diagnosis of a certain disease than on the legitimacy of a certain Law. The concept of *ijmā'* has always implied the consensus of those qualified in matters of Law combined with an inner interaction with the whole of the community whose results are felt only gradually.

As for *qiyās* it means essentially to use human reason to compare an existing situation with one for which legislation already exists. If the Quran has banned wine it means that by analogy it has also banned any form of alcoholic drink whose effect is like wine, namely one which causes intoxication. The use of *qiyās* again is not a licence for rationalism but an exercising of reason within the context of the revealed truths which are the basis of the *Sharī'ah* and the prophetic utterances and practices which have made these truths known and have clarified them for the Muslim community.

Both *ijmā'* and *qiyās* are closely connected to the function of the *'ulamā'* as authorities on Law, of those who having spent their lives studying this particular subject are in a position to pass judgment upon it. There is no priesthood in Islam and every Muslim can perform the functions which in other religions are placed in the hands of the priesthood. But to pass judgement upon the Law is not the right of every Muslim for no other reason than that not everyone is scientifically qualified to do so. Everyone cannot pass judgments upon the *Sharī'ah* for the same reason that everyone cannot give an opinion on astronomy or medicine unless he be qualified in these fields by having studied them. The *'ulamā'* are the custodians of the Law only because they have undertaken the necessary studies and mastered the required disciplines to make them acquainted with its teachings.

Historically, the four above-mentioned principles brought about the formation of the Law in a complex process all of whose details are not well known. As far as the meaning of the *Sharī'ah* for Muslims is concerned this history, as already pointed out, is not of major importance. Yet, since so much attention is paid today to the history of a subject rather than the subject itself, it is necessary to outline briefly the process through which the *Sharī'ah* became codified.

Many of the verses of the Quran are concerned with questions of Law but not all the injunctions of the *Sharī'ah* are explicitly stated in it. About eighty verses are directly connected with specific aspects of the Law. For example, regulations about marriage, divorce and inheritance are very clearly formulated while many other questions are only implicitly stated. There are many universal statements which needed further explanation before they could become specific guides for human action. This explanation and clarification was provided for the most part by the Prophet whose lifetime marks the first and most important period in the process of the codification of the *Sharī'ah*.

The Prophet, as we have already pointed out, was the interpreter *par excellence* of the teachings of the Quran and participated himself in the formation of the *Sharī'ah*. His manner of applying the tenets of Islam to particular instances marked the first phase in the life of the *Sharī'ah* in human society and inaugurated the life of a new society which was moulded by its teachings. This is particularly true of the Medina community where the Prophet broke the pre-existing tribal bonds and established the new Islamic order setting up precedents which have served as a model for all later Muslim jurists.

This unique period in Islamic history was followed by the rule of the first four caliphs, usually called the 'Orthodox caliphs' (*al-khulafā' al-rāshidūn*), as far as Sunni Islam is concerned, and the rule of 'Alī, the fourth of these caliphs and the first Imam, according to the perspective of Shi'ism. During this period the teachings of the Quran and the precedent of the

Prophet were applied not only to conditions that had existed before but to new situations brought about by the rapid spread of Islam outside the homogeneous atmosphere of Arabia. The conquest of parts of the Byzantine empire and the overthrow of the Sassanid empire provided many new problems to whose solution the earlier established principles were applied by men all of whom had been companions of the Prophet, by men whose interest was more in serving Islam than in serving any worldly power. During this period therefore many procedures were established which also became incorporated into the body of the Law.

With the establishment of the Umayyads a new situation arose, one in which a powerful state ruling from Central Asia to Spain and faced with unprecedented administrative and financial problems was interested first and foremost in preserving its political dominion over a vast territory. From the point of view of statesmanship the Umayyads performed a remarkable task of keeping the empire together but from the religious point of view their rule marks a definite falling away from the earlier period. They were not concerned, like the early caliphs, with preserving the Divine Law and applying it. They were interested first and foremost with ruling and administrating the new empire. They dealt with most questions of Law from the point of view of expediency.

During the nearly hundred years of Umayyad rule the responsibility of preserving and administering the *Sharīʿah* lay upon the shoulders of individual judges (*qāḍīs*) who were the real interpreters of the Law at this time. There are records of them, especially those of Egypt, contained in the chronicles of al-Kindī. These sources reveal how these judges dealt with questions of law on a day-to-day basis, trying to apply the precedents of earlier Muslim generations, and especially the Quran and *Ḥadīth*, to whatever new situation confronted them.

But there was a reaction on the part of the religious community—Sunni and Shiʿah alike—against the practices of the Umayyads which, of course, contributed greatly to their downfall. Towards the end of Umayyad period everyone realized that the Muslim community and especially the State were moving away from Islamic ideals. The religious conscience of the whole community—and especially the Shiʿah who had never accepted

Umayyad rule—reacted against the practices of the State and with the coming of the Abbasids there was a sudden burst of activity for the purification of political and social practices and the codification of the Divine Law as established in the Quran and *Ḥadīth*.

It was at this crucial stage that several men of great genius and religious integrity came upon the scene to codify the Law. Because of the vastness of the Islamic community a judge in Khurasan was not faced with the same daily problems as one in the Maghrib, nor one in Kufa with the same situation as that confronted in Medina. These last two cities were particularly important in the development of the Law. Medina was an Arab city where some of the old tribal and family bonds still survived, whereas Kufa had come into being during the Islamic period. There, Arabs, Persians and local Aramaic people had come together to form a new society which was held together by the common ideals of Islam. Yet, both cities had been sites of early Muslim rule and provided the required background for anyone who wanted to study the practices of the early Muslim community. From these two cities in fact arose the first two founders of Sunni law, Ibn Mālik from Medina and Abū Ḥanīfah from Kufa. These men established schools of law by making a careful study of the Quran and *Ḥadīth* and the practices of the earlier generations. Basing themselves on meticulous study, they composed compendia of Law in which the teachings of the *Sharī'ah* as they pertain to all aspects of life were delineated and systematized.

There was at this point still a need to have the principles and methods of jurisprudence systematized and a final form given to the process of promulgating the Law. Such a need was fulfilled by al-Shāfi'ī whose particular genius in this domain gave to Sunni Islam the most satisfying and one might say beautiful method of jurisprudence. Al-Shāfi'ī made it clear that the *Ḥadīth* was not only an aid to understanding the Quran but a source of the *Sharī'ah* itself. The clarification of the role of *Ḥadīth* in the *Sharī'ah* is due to him more than to anyone else, as are the respective positions of *ijmā'* and *qiyās*. With al-Shāfi'ī Islamic jurisprudence found its most complete and lasting systematization.

In the tradition of al-Shāfi'ī, who founded the third school of

Sunni law, there grew students each of whom emphasized a certain aspect of the sources of the *Sharī'ah* such as Ibn Ḥanbal, who relied essentially on prophetic *Ḥadīth* after the Quran and discounted *ijmā'* and *qiyās*, and Dā'ūd ibn Khalaf who believed that the external (*ẓāhirī*) meaning of the Quran alone should be followed and founded the Zahirite school. The school of Ibn Ḥanbal became the fourth accepted school of Sunni law with its characteristic disdain of rationalist methods and complete reliance upon *Ḥadīth* literature while the Zahirite school gradually disappeared.

The four important schools of Sunni law, the Malikite, Hanafite, Shafi'ite and Hanbalite, that constitute the accepted schools of *Sharī'ah* to the present day, thus came into being in the third Islamic century. Of these, the one with the least number of followers is the Hanbalite school which for long had its centre in Egypt and Syria and from whose background the Wahhaḅi movement began. The Shafi'ite school has always been strong in Egypt and to a certain extent in Syria. The Malikite school is completely dominant in North Africa and its followers constitute the most homogeneous body in the realm of Sunni Law. As for the Hanafi school, it was the official school of the Ottomans and is widespread in Turkey, the eastern part of the Arab world and the Indo–Pakistani sub-continent.

As far as Law in the Shi'ah world is concerned its formation goes back to the fifth and sixth Imams, especially the sixth Imam Ja'far al-Ṣādiq so that Twelve-imam Shi'ite Law is often called Ja'fari Law. There is one difference with Sunni law in that in both Twelve-imam Shi'ism and Isma'ilism the Imams are the interpreters of the Law and their words and sayings form a part of the *Ḥadīth* literature in addition to the utterances of the Prophet although the distinction between the two is preserved. The Law is therefore, in principle, continuously being made in as much as the Imam is always alive. The Imam of Isma'ilism continues to live on earth from generation to generation while in Twelve-imam Shi'ism the Imam is in occultation (*ghaibah*) although he is alive and rules the world.

In Twelve-imam Shi'ism those who have attained a high stage of proficiency in the science of the Law and possess the other traditional requirements become *mujtahids*, that is, those who can practice *ijtihād* or exercise their opinion in questions of Law. They are living interpreters of the Law who interpret it in the absence of the Imam and in his name. Every Shi'ite believer must follow a living *mujtahid* whose duty it is to apply and interpret the Law from generation to generation. The gate of *ijtihād* has been closed in the Sunni world since the formation of the four schools of Law whereas in Shi'ism the gate must of necessity be always open. But of course this does not by any means detract from the immutable and transcendent nature of the *Sharī'ah*. It only means that in each generation the Law should be applied to the new circumstances that are faced. The practice of *ijtihād* in the spirit of Islam does not mean to change the Law to suit the convenience of men but to face and solve every new situation and problem in conformity with the teachings of the *Sharī'ah* by applying those teachings to newly arisen problems. Shi'ism is there to prove that *ijtihād* in the true sense does not by any means imply the abandonment of the Divine Law to human whims and fancies as some would like to make it today.

As far as the specific teachings of the *Sharī'ah* are concerned the Sunni and Shi'ite schools are nearly the same except in the question of inheritance where, according to Shi'ite Law, in certain cases the female line inherits more than in Sunni law. Otherwise, there is little disagreement between them. As for the different Sunni schools each emphasizes a certain aspect of the Law. For example, the Hanafis rely more on *qiyās* and the Hanbalis on *Ḥadīth* but the deviations are slight and one can go from one school to another without any difficulty. It is also of interest to cite in this context the attempt of the Persian king Nādir Shah who two centuries ago tried to make Ja'fari Law a fifth school of Law in Islam and thereby bring about a concordance between Sunnism and Shi'ism. Mainly for political reasons, however, his plan was not accepted by the Ottoman caliph and did not bear any fruit. A similar attempt is being made in certain quarters today as seen by the teaching of Ja'fari Law at al-Azhar and different movements for the rapprochement between Sunnism and Shi'ism.

More essential than the process of codification of the *Sharī'ah* is its actual content and substance. The *Sharī'ah* possesses the quality of totality and comprehensiveness. It encompasses the whole of man's life so that from the Islamic point of view there is no domain that lies outside of it even if such an ideal is not easy to realize completely in human society. The lack of words in Arabic, Persian and other languages of the Islamic people for temporal or secular matters is due to this total nature of the *Sharī'ah*.

Nevertheless, the Divine Law is comprised of branches depending on the particular aspect of life with which it is concerned. Some of the traditional scholars have divided it into two branches, one dealing with acts of worship (*'ibādāt*) and the other treating of transactions (*mu'āmalāt*). This classical division has led certain modernists to the conclusion that the first part of the *Sharī'ah* can be preserved while the second can be secularized or at least changed as one sees fit. From the point of view of the *Sharī'ah*, however, these two branches cannot be completely divorced from each other. Such acts of worship as the congregational prayer or fasting have a definite social aspect and involve the whole of the community, whereas how one deals in the market-place directly affects the quality and intensity of one's worship. There is no way to separate completely what concerns the relation between man and God from man's relation to other men. The two are inextricably intertwined and the spirit of the *Sharī'ah* is precisely to preserve the unity of human life, albeit it has branches which apply to different domains, individual as well as social. To understand the content of the *Sharī'ah* it is therefore best to analyse its injunctions as they pertain to each particular domain of human life.

Politically, the *Sharī'ah* contains definitive teachings which form the basis of Islamic political theory. In the Islamic view God is the only legislator. Man has no power to make laws; he must obey the laws God has sent for him. Therefore, any ideal government from the point of view of the *Sharī'ah* is devoid of legislative power in the Islamic sense. The function of the political ruler is not to legislate laws but to execute them. The cardinal fact is the presence of a Divine Law which should be administered in society.

As to the question of who the ruler in Islamic society should be, Sunnism and Shi'ism differ. For Twelve-imam Shi'ism there is no perfect government in the absence of the *Mahdī* or Twelfth Imam. In such a situation a monarchy or sultanate that rules with the consent of the *'ulamā'* is the best possible form of government in circumstances which by definition cannot be perfect. In Sunnism it is the caliphate that is considered as the legitimate form of rule. The caliph is the *khalīfah* or vice-gerent not of God but of His Prophet and then only of that aspect of the function of the Prophet which was concerned with administering the Divine Law. The function of the caliph is to guard and administer the *Sharī'ah*, and he stands as the symbol of the rule of the *Sharī'ah* over human society. Islam is not technically speaking a theocracy but a nomocracy, that is a society ruled by a Divine Law.

Since there is only one Islamic people or 'Muḥammadan Community' (*ummah muḥammadīyah*), naturally there should be only one caliph who should rule over the whole *ummah*. But what is essential to the preservation of the unity of Islamic community is not so much the number of caliphs as the *Sharī'ah* itself. When one glances over pages of Islamic history it becomes clear that after the first four caliphs, the Umayyads were mostly like secular rulers. Some like Yazīd even broke the tenets of the *Sharī'ah* in their personal lives and many of them were tyrants. But the difference between them and a modern tyrant is that in the Umayyad period the *Sharī'ah* was nevertheless applied while in modern times in many a land the attempt is being made to destroy the *Sharī'ah* itself.

After the Umayyad period the Western lands of Islam refused to pay allegiance to the Abbasids and soon there were several rulers and even caliphs in the Muslim world. Moreover, with the destruction of the Abbasid caliphate by Hulagu even the symbolic political unity of Islam was destroyed. But throughout these changes the *'ulamā'*, and also the Sufi orders in the eastern lands of Islam, succeeded in guarding the *Sharī'ah* even before the Mongol onslaught. Therefore, in all these instances the unity of Islam was preserved by virtue of the preservation of the *Sharī'ah*. Although there was no longer a single political power ruling over the whole Muslim world the same laws were being administered in the courts of Morocco as in Northern India. The rule of Divine Law continued to preserve the unity of the community and to guarantee its Islamic nature.

Of course during the course of Islamic history Sunni political theory itself was revised in the light of events. With the appearance of powerful kings or sultans who soon became the real rulers of the land and possessed more power than the caliphs, a new situation arose. During the Seljuq period the Sunni political theoreticians recognized instead of the dual structure of *Sharī'ah* and caliph, a tripartite political pattern in which there was the *Sharī'ah*, the caliph who symbolized its rule, and the sultan who actually ran the affairs of state. Some of the Muslims in India even continued to recite the name of the Abbasid caliph in the Friday sermons, as a symbol of the rule of the *Sharī'ah*, after the Abbasid caliphate itself had been destroyed. The essential element that survived throughout the centuries was the *Sharī'ah* so that the essential nomocratic nature of Islamic society was maintained and political turmoils, even on as colossal a scale as the Mongol invasion, were not able to destroy the unity of the Islamic community which the *Sharī'ah* both inculcated and preserved.

In the domain of economics, also, the *Sharī'ah* contains both specific instructions and general principles. It legislates certain forms of taxation such as *zakāt*—and for the Shi'ah also *khums*—which have been paid over the ages by devout Muslims. But in general the Sharī'ite laws of Taxation have not been the only ones to have been applied. Look at land tax for example. In Syria, from Umayyad times, taxes were collected according to Byzantine precedents and in Persia in accordance with Sassanid laws. Even after the Mongol invasion in certain villages land tax was collected according to Mongolian regulations.

In a more general sense the economic teachings of the *Sharī'ah* are based on the respect for private property and, at the same time, opposition to extreme concentration of wealth in the hands of a single person or group. Usury is specifically forbidden and the paying of *zakāt* itself has the function of 'purifying' one's wealth and also distributing some of it among the rest of the members of society through the 'Muslim public treasury' (*bait māl al-muslimīn*). The emphasis on the sacrosanct nature of private property is also clearly stated in the Quran. In fact the economic legislation of the Quran could not be applied were there to be no private property. According to the *Sharī'ah* man is given the right to own property by God and the possession of property is necessary for the fulfilment of his soul in this world provided he keeps within the teachings of the

Sharī'ah. Those who interpret the teachings of Islam in a purely socialistic sense oppose the very text of the Quran which instructs man as to what he should do with his possessions. The Quran could not legislate about property if it did not accept the legitimacy of private property.

Altogether of all the aspects of the *Sharī'ah* its economic teachings are perhaps those that have been least perfectly realized throughout Islamic history. But they have always stood as the ideal to be reached although they cannot be fully achieved considering the imperfections of human nature. The general spirit of Sharī'ite teachings, however, is deeply ingrained in the economic life of Muslims. Although specific forms of taxation may not have been followed and non-Sharī'ite taxes may have been levied, the general economic principles of the *Sharī'ah* have been realized to a great extent throughout history among traditional merchants and in craft guilds.

As far as the social teachings of the *Sharī'ah* are concerned they comprise a vast subject which one cannot treat fully here. Altogether the *Sharī'ah* envisages a fluid society, not in the modern proletarian sense, but in a traditional one. Before the rise of Islam there was an Arab aristocracy as well as a Persian one. Islam, by remoulding society, did not destroy quality but made faith itself the criterion of man's worth according to the well-known Quranic verse, 'Lo! the noblest of you, in the sight of Allah, is the best in conduct.' (XLIX, 13)

(ان اكرمكم عند الله اتقيكم).

By upholding the primary value of religion Islam made it possible for man to climb the scale of society through mastery in the religious sciences. A person who was gifted could become one of the *'ulamā'* and enjoy a respect greater than that afforded to a prince. Likewise, the Sufi orders have preserved a spiritual hierarchy in which the rank of a person depends upon his spiritual qualifications and not upon his social standing. The Sufi masters and saints have been the most venerated of men, respected by king and beggar alike.

In fact up to modern times not only has the religious path of climbing the social scale been well preserved but learning itself has been a way to advance one's social position. Even if learning and education be secular today, they continue to bear the prestige of religious education in the eyes of Muslim society at large. There are numerous men who hold positions of power in various Muslim lands whose father or grandfather may have been simple store keepers who sent their children to school and the children through their own capabilities were able to take maximum advantage of the education offered to them and have become leading figures in society. This fact is as true of Islamic society throughout its history as it is now. How many wazīrs and even kings has the Islamic world seen who became the most powerful figures in the land through their own capabilities? The *Sharī'ah* by stressing the quality of religious faith as the criterion of human value created a fluid society, one which, however, was not quantitative and did not suppress quality in terms of a supposed egalitarianism as we find in so many contemporary societies.

One could in fact say, quoting a contemporary sage, that Islam 'is a democracy of married monks', that is, a society in which equality exists in the religious sense in that all men are priests and stand equally before God as his vice-gerent on earth. But he who is more able to realize his real nature and function is qualitatively superior to one for whom being in the human state is only accidental. The equality of men is not in their qualities, which obviously are different from one person to the next, but in that for all men the possibility of realizing their theomorphic nature and fulfilling the purpose of human existence is ever present.

From the point of view of social structure, the teachings of the *Sharī'ah* emphasize the role of the family as the unit of society, family in the extended sense not in its atomized modern form. The greatest social achievement of the Prophet in Medina was precisely in breaking the existing tribal bonds and substituting religious ones which were connected on the one hand with the totality of the Muslim community and on the other with the family. The Muslim family is the miniature of the whole of Muslim society and its firm basis. In it the man or father functions as the imam in accordance with the patriarchal nature of Islam. The religious responsibility of the family rests upon his shoulders. He is in a sense the priest in that he can perform the rites which in other religions are reserved for the priestly class. In the family the father upholds the tenets of the religion and his authority symbolizes that of God in the world. The man is in fact respected in the family precisely because of the sacerdotal function that he fulfils. The rebellion of Muslim women in certain quarters of Islamic society came when men themselves ceased to fulfil their religious function and lost their virile and patriarchal character. By becoming themselves effeminate they caused the ensuing reaction of revolt among certain women who no longer felt the authority of religion upon themselves.

The traditional family is also the unit of stability in society, and the four wives that a Muslim can marry, like the four-sided Ka'bah, symbolize this stability. Many have not understood why such a family structure is permitted in Islam and attack Islam for it, as if polygamy belongs to Islam alone. Here again modernism carries with it the prejudice of Christianity against polygamy to the extent that some have even gone so far as to call it immoral and prefer prostitution to a social pattern which minimizes all promiscuous relations to the extent possible. The problem of the attitude of Western observers is not as important as that segment of modernized Muslim society which itself cannot understand the teachings of the *Sharī'ah* on this point, simply because it uses as criteria categories borrowed from the modern West.

There is no doubt that in a small but significant segment of Muslim society today there is a revolt of women against traditional Islamic society. In every civilization a reaction comes always against an existing force or action. The Renaissance adoration of nature is a direct reaction to the dominant medieval Christian conception of nature as a domain of darkness and evil to be shunned. In Islam also the very patriarchal and masculine nature of the tradition makes the revolt of those women who have become aggressively modernized more violent and virulent than let us say in Hinduism where the maternal element has always been strong. What many modernized Muslim women are doing in rebelling against the traditional Muslim family structure is to rebel against fourteen centuries of Islam itself, although many may not be aware of the inner forces that drive them on. It is the patriarchal nature of Islam that makes the reaction of some modernized women today so vehement. Although very limited in number they are in fact, more than

Muslim men, thirsting for all things Western. They seek to become modernized in their dress and habits with an impetuosity which would be difficult to understand unless one considers the deep psychological factors involved.

From the Islamic point of view the question of the equality of men and women is meaningless. It is like discussing the equality of a rose and jasmine. Each has its own perfume, colour, shape and beauty. Man and woman are not the same; each has particular features and characteristics. Women are not equal to men. But then neither are men equal to women. Islam envisages their roles in society not as competing but as complementary. Each has certain duties and functions in accordance with his or her nature and constitutition.

Man possesses certain privileges such as social authority and mobility against which he has to perform many heavy duties. First of all he bears all economic responsibility. It is his duty to support his family completely even if his wife is rich and despite the fact that she is economically completely independent. A woman in traditional Islamic society does not have to worry about earning a living. There is always the larger family structure in which she can find a place and take refuge from social and economic pressures even if she has no husband or father. In the extended family system a man often supports not only his wife, but also his mother, sister, aunts, in-laws and sometimes even cousins and more distant relatives. Therefore, in city life the necessity of having to find a job at all costs and having to bear the economic pressure of life is lifted from the shoulders of women. As for the countryside the family is itself the economic unit and the work is achieved by the larger family or tribal unit together.

Secondly, a woman does not have to find a husband for herself. She does not have to display her charms and make the thousand and one plans through which she hopes to attract a future mate. The terrible anxiety of having to find a husband and of missing the opportunity if one does not try hard enough at the right moment is spared the Muslim woman. Being able to remain more true to her own nature she can afford to sit at home and await the suitable match. This usually leads to a marriage which being based on the sense of religious duty and enduring family and social correspondence between the two sides is more lasting and ends much more rarely in divorce than the marriages which are based on the sentiments of the moment that often do not develop into more permanent relationships.

Thirdly, the Muslim woman is spared direct military and political responsibility although in rare cases there have been women warriors. This point may appear as a deprivation to some but in the light of the real needs of feminine nature it is easy to see that for most women such duties weigh heavily upon them. Even in modern societies which through the equalitarian process have tried to equate men and women, as if there were no difference in the two natures, women are usually spared the military draft except in extreme circumstances.

In return for these privileges which the woman receives she has also certain responsibilities of which the most important is to provide a home for her family and to bring up her children properly. In the home the woman rules as queen and a Muslim man is in a sense the guest of his wife at home. The home and the larger family structure in which she lives are for the Muslim woman her world. To be cut off from it would be like being cut off from the world or like dying. She finds the meaning of her existence in this extended family structure which is constructed so as to give her the maximum possibility of realizing her basic needs and fulfilling herself.

The *Sharīʻah* therefore envisages the role of men and women according to their nature which is complementary. It gives the man the privilege of social and political authority and movement for which he has to pay by bearing heavy responsibilities, by protecting his family from all the forces and pressures of society, economic and otherwise. Although a master in the world at large and the priest of his own family, man acts in his home as one who recognizes the rule of his wife in this domain and respects it. Through mutual understanding and the realization of the responsibilities that God has placed on each other's shoulders, the Muslim man and woman are able to fulfil their personal lives and create a firm family unit which is the basic structure of Muslim society.

Besides its political, economic and social teachings, the *Sharīʻah* concerns itself with what is most essential to every religion, namely the relation between man and God. The most central aspect of the *Sharīʻah* is concerned with the rites or acts of worship which every Muslim must perform and which constitute the ritual and devotional practices of Muslims. Of these rites the most important are the daily prayers (*ṣalāt*) which, as we have seen, are the prop of religion. No act in the *Sharīʿah* is as essential as the performance of these prayers. They are preceded by a call (*adhān*) and ablutions (*wuḍūʾ*), which mean not only a physical purification of the body but the purification of the soul as well. Through them the dross of separative existence is washed away and man becomes ready to stand before God. He suddenly feels as if his body is infused with light and is re-instated in its Edenic purity.

The ablutions are followed by the prayers which take place, as is well known, at sunrise, noon, afternoon, sunset and night. The continuous repetition of the prayers at particular moments of the day and night serves to break in a systematic fashion this dream of negligence in which man lives. Man lives in a dream immersed in the world and forgetful of God. The canonical prayers interrupt this dream at least a few times each day. For a few moments they pull man out of that stream of thoughts and sensual impressions that is the world and make him stand face to face before God. Thus man realizes through these prayers his theomorphic nature at least as long as he is performing the prayers. They become for him a precious shelter in the storm of life. Only the saint is able to live in prayer continuously and be awake at all times.

The canonical prayers should not be identified with individual prayers which are often added afterwards. In the canonical prayers man stands before God as the representative of all creatures. He prays for and in the name of all beings. That is why, as we have said, the verses of the chapter 'the Opening' (*al-Fātiḥah*) which constitute the heart of the canonical prayers are all in the first person plural not singular. Man recites, 'Thee (alone) *we* worship' not 'Thee I worship'. In these prayers man fulfils his function as the vice-gerent of God on earth and prays for all beings.

The canonical prayers are the heart of the *Sharīʿah* and they are obligatory. Such is not the case of the Friday congregational prayers which are highly recommended especially in Sunni Islam but are not obligatory. The Friday prayers serve the function of creating social cohesion among believers and also of providing an opportunity for religious teachers to deliver moral and religious lessons. They have also always been connected with political authority and the name of the ruler mentioned in the Friday sermon has traditionally carried much prestige. Despite their great importance, however, the Friday prayers are not on the same level as the daily canonical prayers that can be performed at home or in a mosque or in nature for that matter, nature which is the primordial mosque created by God and provides the perfect background for worship. The Friday prayers must be in a congregation and are usually held in a mosque; the canonical prayers can be performed anywhere and are absolutely obligatory upon every Muslim.

After the *ṣalāt* or canonical prayers, the second basic act of worship that is obligatory for every Muslim—except the sick and the traveller—is fasting during the holy month of Ramaḍān. Fasting is a recommended act in Islam but during this particular month it becomes a religious duty. The fasting from the first sign of dawn to sunset is not only abstention from food, drink and sexual pleasures but also from all evil thoughts and deeds. It is a rigorous means of self-purification. It is as if one were to wear the armour of God against the world and introduce the purity of death within his body, that purity and incorruptibility which are like a crystal, hard and immutable yet transparent before light.

The ordeal of fasting has its spiritual significance first and foremost in that man consciously obeys a Divine command. But in addition it is the means by which man pulls the reins of his animal desires and realizes that he is more than an animal. As long as man follows his passions and inclinations completely he differs little from the animals except that they are innocent and true to their nature while man is not. It is only when man exerts his spiritual will through asceticism against his animal inclinations that he realizes his higher nature. Even the sensual enjoyments become heightened through denial. The full satisfaction of the senses dulls them. Therefore, the experience of this month of fasting makes man more appreciative of the gifts that God has bestowed upon him and which he usually takes for granted. It is also a period of exercising charity in which man shares with those who have less material blessings than he. But most of all it is a month of purification, a month rich in its graces, one during which the Quran itself was revealed, the 'Night of Power' (*lailat al-qadr*) falling on one of the last odd nights of Ramaḍān. During this month the gates of heaven are more open and the Muslim individual as well as the community are able to purify themselves with the aid of Divine grace and renew the spiritual energy of society.

The pilgrimage to Mecca (*ḥajj*) is another obligatory act which may, however, be undertaken only when certain conditions are fulfilled. A man, if he has the sufficient means, should once in his lifetime make the pilgrimage to Mecca which for Islam is the centre of the world. The *ḥajj* with all the difficulties that it entailed and still entails, despite modern conveniences, is also a means of purification. Man journeys to the Centre, to the house of God, there asking pardon for his sins and being purified through his repentance and the performance of the rites. Henceforth, he should try to live a devout life and when he returns to his homeland he brings the purity and grace (*barakah*) of the house of God with him. Something of the Centre is thus disseminated in the periphery and through this yearly act the whole of the Muslim community is purified.

The *ḥajj* is also a remarkable way of achieving social integration. Every year over the centuries Muslims from all parts of the world have met and exchanged both ideas and goods. They have realized the vastness of the Islamic world and have come to know the other parts of it better. The *ḥajj* has also played a role of great importance in the dissemination of knowledge from one part of the Islamic world to another, to the extent that a modern Western scholar has called it the first international scientific congress in history. But its importance is most of all to unify the Muslim community and spread the purity which lies at its heart to its limbs and organs.

As for the other major rites prescribed by the *Sharīʻah*, *zakāt* and *jihād* or holy war are the most important. The first is a way of paying 'God's due' for whatever we receive. It is thus a form of sacrifice (*sacer-facere*—to make sacred), which purifies and makes lawful what one spends, giving to man's economic life a religious sanction. The *jihād* in the external sense is an occasional activity not like others which are always practised. Its ever present significance lies in the 'great holy war' which, as we have had occasion to point out before, is a constant war which every Muslim must wage against the evil and disruptive tendencies within himself.

Not only the *jihād* but every injunction of the *Sharī'ah* has also an inner and spiritual meaning. The *ṣalāt* means to awaken from one's dream of forgetfulness and remember God always, the fast means to die to one's passionate self and be born in purity, the pilgrimage means to journey from the surface to the centre of one's being for, as so many Sufis have said, the heart is the spiritual Ka'bah. The *zakāt* also implies spiritual generosity and nobility. This inner meaning does not negate the external teachings of the *Sharī'ah* but complements and fulfils its spiritual aim. That is why the *Sharī'ah* is the necessary and sufficient basis for the spiritual life. Every man must accept the *Sharī'ah* in order to be a Muslim. And the highest spiritual castle in Islam, that of the greatest sages and saints, is based on the firm foundation provided by the *Sharī'ah*. Man cannot aspire to the spiritual life, to walking upon the path to God (*Ṭarīqah*), without participating in the *Sharī'ah*.

Certain modernists over the past century have tried to change the *Sharī'ah*, to reopen the gate of *ijtihād*, with the aim of incorporating modern practices into the Law and limiting the functioning of the *Sharī'ah* to personal life. All of these activities emanate from a particular attitude of spiritual weakness *vis-à-vis* the world and a surrender to the world. Those who are conquered by such a mentality want to make the *Sharī'ah* 'conform to the times' which means to the whims and fancies of men and the ever changing human nature which has made 'the times'. They do not realize that it is the *Sharī'ah* according to which society should be modelled not vice versa. They do not realize that those who practiced *ijtihād* before were devout Muslims who put the interest of Islam before the world and never surrendered its principles to expediency.

In the Islamic perspective God has revealed the *Sharī'ah* to man so that through it he can reform himself and his society. It is man who is in need of reform not divinely revealed religion. The presence of the *Sharī'ah* in the world is due to the compassion of God for his creatures so that he has sent an all encompassing Law for them to follow and thereby to gain felicity in both this world and the next. The *Sharī'ah* is thus the ideal for human society and the individual. It provides meaning for all human activities and integrates human life. It is the norm for the perfect social and human life and the necessary basis for all flights of the spirit from the periphery to the Centre. To live according to the *Sharī'ah* is to live according to the Divine Will, according to a norm which God has willed for man.

Suggestions for further reading

Agnides, N. P., *Mohammedan Theories of Finance*, Lahore, Premier Book House, 1961. A thorough and objective analysis of Muslim economic theories and practices.

Ahmad, M., *Economics of Islam*, Lahore, Muhammad Ashraf, 1947. The best explanation of economic principles from the orthodox Muslim view.

Arnold, T. W., *The Preaching of Islam*, Lahore, Shirkat-i Qualam, 1956. A still outstanding work on the history of the spread of Islam over the world.

Asad, M., *Islam at the Crossroads*, Lahore, Muhammad Ashraf, 1947. An excellent study of the significance of the *Sharī'ah* in the light of the problems that the Muslim world faces in the modern world.

Baillie, N. B., *A Digest of Moohummudan Law*, London, Smith, Elder & Co., 1887. The English translation of *Sharā'i' al-islām*, one of the most authoritative Shi'ite works of law.

Coulson, N. J., *Islamic Surveys, 2, A History of Islamic Law*, Edinburgh, University Press, 1964. A handy and useful survey of the *Sharī'ah* and its history with a good bibliography but following the usual view of orientalists towards *Ḥadīth* and the formation of the Divine Law.

Fyzee, A. A. A., *Outlines of Muhammadan Law*, London, Oxford University Press, 1955. A handbook of Muslim Law, both Sunni and Shi'ite, outlining the teachings of the Law as especially administered in the Indo-Pakistani subcontinent.

Gardet, L., *La Cité musulmane, vie sociale et politique*, Paris, J. Vrin, 1961. Perhaps the best European source on Muslim social and political ideals with a certain amount of comparison with Christian beliefs.

Gibb, H. A. R., *Mohammadanism*, Chapter VI. A simple yet clear account of the nature and function of the *Sharī'ah*.

—"Law and Religion in Islam," *Judaism and Christianity*, ed. E. I. J. Rosenthal, Vol. III, pp. 145–170, London, Shelden Press, 1938. A good survey of the significance of the *Sharī'ah* in Islam.

Goldziher, I., "The Principles of Law in Islam," *The Historian's History of the World*, ed. H. S. Williams, Vol. III, pp. 294–304, London, *The Times*, 1908. A clear statement of the principles of Islamic Law.

—*Vorlesungen über den Islam*, Heidelberg, Winter, 1925; French trans. by F. Arin, *Le Dogme et la loi de l'Islam*, Paris, Geuthner, 1920. An influential work on the contents of the *Sharī'ah* and one of the important writings of Western orientalists on this subject.

Hamidullah, M., *The Muslim Conduct of State*, Lahore, Muhammad Ashraf, 1954. A Muslim account of Islamic political theory and practice with special emphasis on the early period of Islam.

Khadduri, M. (trans.), *Islamic Jurisprudence, Shāfi'ī's Risāla*, Baltimore, John Hopkins Press, 1961. A good English translation of the well-known treatise of al-Shāfi'ī which is the basis of all jurisprudence in Sunni Islam.

Khadduri, M. and Liebesny, H. J., (ed.), *Law in the Middle East*, I, Washington, Middle East Institute, 1955. A survey of law in its foundations and daily application in the Middle East today.

Levy, R., *The Social Structure of Islam*, Cambridge, University Press, 1962. A well-written study of the social structure of Islam with many chapters devoted to different aspects of the *Sharī'ah* and meant as an introduction to the whole of Islam and its civilization.

Macdonald, D. B., *Development of Muslim Theology, Jurisprudence and Constitutional Theory*, New York, Macmillan, 1903. Although somewhat out of date still a useful outline of Muslim Law and theology.

Mahmasani, S., *The Philosophy of Jurisprudence in Islam*, trans. F. Ziadeh, Leiden, E. J. Brill, 1962. An outstanding analysis of the principles and philosophy of Islamic jurisprudence based on traditional sources and practices.

Merchant, M. V., *A Book of Quranic Laws*, Lahore, Muhammad Ashraf, 1960. The laws outlined in the Quran are enumerated and discussed as seen by a Muslim.

Nasr, S. H., *Islamic Studies, Essays on Law and Society, the Sciences, Philosophy and Sufism*, Beirut, Librairie du Liban, 1965, Part I. A discussion of some of the problems that the spread of secularism poses for the *Sharī'ah* and an evaluation of modern threats to the *Sharī'ah* from the view of traditional Islam.

Roberts, R., *The Social Laws of the Quran*, London, Williams and Norgate, 1925. An outline of those aspects of the *Sharī'ah* that are mentioned in the Quran.

Rosenthal, E. I. J., *Political Thought in Medieval Islam*, Cambridge, University Press, 1958. A well-documented and sympathetic survey of Islamic political theory in which both theological and philosophical sources are examined.

Santillana, D., *Istituzioni di diritto musulmano malichita, con riguardo anche al sistema sciafiita*, 2 vols., Rome, Istituto per l'Oriente, 1926–38. The most thorough and detailed analysis of Islamic law in a European language.

Schacht, J., *An Introduction to Islamic Law*, Oxford, Clarendon Press, 1964. A detailed survey of Islamic law containing both a historical and a systematic analysis and an outstanding bibliography by one of the leading European students of the *Sharī'ah* who, however, like most other orientalists does not accept the traditional Muslim view of the origin and role of the Divine Law.

Siddiqi, A. H., *Caliphate and Sultanate*, Karachi, Jamiyat Faleh Publications, 1963. A contemporary orthodox Muslim discussion of the caliphate and sultanate.

de Zayas, F., *The Law and Philosophy of Zakat*, Damascus, al-Jadidah Press, 1960. A thorough study of *zakāt* in both its social application and religious significance from the Muslim point of view.

CHAPTER V

The Ṭarīqah The Spiritual Path and its Quranic Roots

The *Ṭarīqah* or Spiritual Path which is usually known as *Taṣawwuf* or Sufism is the inner and esoteric dimension of Islam and like the *Sharī'ah* has its roots in the Quran and prophetic practice. Being the heart of the Islamic message it, like the physical heart, is hidden from external view, although again like the heart it is the inner source of life and the centre which coordinates inwardly the whole religious organism of Islam. The *Ṭarīqah* is the most subtle and difficult aspect of Islam to understand at the same time that its external effect is to be seen in many manifestations of Islamic society and civilization. Our task in this chapter is not to discuss the manifestations of Sufism in Islamic history but to delineate the essential principles of the *Ṭarīqah* and its Quranic roots. It is to outline the features that characterize Islamic spirituality of which the *Ṭarīqah* is the custodian and for which it provides the means of realization.

As pointed out in the previous chapter, the *Sharī'ah* is the Divine Law by virtue of whose acceptance man becomes a Muslim. Only by living according to it can man gain that equilibrium which is the necessary basis for entering upon the Path or *Ṭarīqah*. Only a man who can walk on flat ground can hope to climb a mountain. Without participation in the *Sharī'ah* the life of the *Ṭarīqah* would be impossible and in fact the latter is interwoven in its practices and attitudes with the practices prescribed by the *Sharī'ah*.

Some of the traditional Sufi masters, especially those of the Shādhilīyah order, have used the geometric symbol of a circle to depict the relation between these fundamental dimensions of Islam. From any point in space there can be generated a circle and an indefinite number of radii which connect every point of the circumference of the circle of the Centre. The circumference is the *Sharī'ah* whose totality comprises the whole of the Muslim community. Every Muslim by virtue of accepting the Divine Law is as a point standing on this circle. The radii symbolize the *Ṭuruq* (plural of *Ṭarīqah*). Each radius is a path from the circumference to the Centre. As the Sufis say there are as many paths to God as there are children of Adam. The *Ṭarīqah*, which exists in many different forms corresponding to different spiritual temperaments and needs of men, is the radius which connects each point to the Centre. It is only by virtue of standing on the circumference, that is, accepting the *Sharī'ah*, that man can discover before him a radius that leads to the Centre. Only in following the *Sharī'ah* does the possibility of having the door of the spiritual life open become realized.

Finally at the Centre there is the *Ḥaqīqah* or Truth which is the source of both the *Ṭarīqah* and the *Sharī'ah*. Just as geometrically the point generates both the radii and the circumference, so does metaphysically the *Ḥaqīqah* create both the *Ṭarīqah* and the *Sharī'ah*, that *Ḥaqīqah* or Centre which is 'everywhere and nowhere'. The Law and the Way have both been brought into being independently by God who is the Truth. And both reflect the Centre in different ways. To participate in the *Sharī'ah* is to live in the reflection of the Centre or Unity, for the circumference is the reflection of the Centre. It is thus the necessary and sufficient cause for living a whole life and being 'saved'. But there are always those whose inner constitution is such that they cannot only live in the reflection of the Centre but must seek to reach It. Their Islam *is* to walk upon the Path towards the Centre. For them the *Ṭarīqah* is providentially the means whereby they can attain that final End or Goal, that *Ḥaqīqah* which is the Origin of all things, from which the integral tradition comprising the Law and the Way or the circumference and radii originate.

Although Islam in its totality has been able to preserve throughout its history a balance between the two dimensions of the Law and the Way, there have been occasionally those who have emphasized one at the expense of the other. There have been those who have denied the radii in favour of the circumference, who have negated the validity of the *Ṭarīqah* in the light of the *Sharī'ah*. Some of them have had the function, as custodians of the *Sharī'ah,* to defend it and its absolute necessity, while on another level they may have accepted or even participated in the *Ṭarīqah* themselves. Such men are called the *'ulamā' al-ẓāhir*, the doctors of the Law, whose duty it is to guard and preserve the teachings of the Sacred Law. Others have gone to the point of negating the Way completely, being satisfied solely with an external interpretation of the religion. They are the superficial (*qishrī*) *'ulamā'* who would break the balance and equilibrium between the exoteric and esoteric dimensions were they to dominate the whole of the Muslim community. But, although as a reaction against the modern West, a certain trend closely connected with such a view has gained ascendency in certain quarters, such a point of view has never prevailed over the total orthodoxy and has remained a peripheral position. For the vast majority of orthodox Muslims, the Sufi remains a devout Muslim who is respected for the depth of his religious life even if all that he does and practices is not known or understood by the rest of the community at large.

On the other hand also there have been those who have tried occasionally to break the balance in favour of the *Ṭarīqah* as if it were possible for the Way to exist in the world without the Law which serves as its outward shield and protects it from the withering influence of the world. In fact so many of the movements which have ended in the creation of a sect or even deviation from and break with the total orthodoxy of Islam have come about as the attempt to exteriorize esotericism without the support of the *Sharī'ah*. In general many a pseudo-religious and devious sect begins from an esoteric background which by breaking the protecting mould of the *Sharī'ah* itself deviates from its original nature, resulting in either relatively harmless small sects or positively harmful pseudo-religions depending on the climate in which such movements grow.

Islam in its totality, however, has been able to preserve this balance between the exoteric and the esoteric or *tafsīr* and *ta'wīl* as far as the Quranic interpretation is concerned. The larger orthodoxy of the Muslim community has always been able to prevail and prevent either the Law from stifling the Way or the Way from breaking the mould of the Law and thereby destroying the equilibrium of Islamic society. The religious and spiritual vitality of Islam has come from the presence of both these dimensions over the ages which together have constituted an integral religious tradition capable of creating a religious society and the norms of the inner spiritual life. According to the well-known Sufi symbol Islam is like a walnut of which the shell is like the *Sharīʻah*, the kernel like the *Ṭarīqah* and the oil which is invisible yet everywhere present, the *Ḥaqīqah*. A walnut without a shell could not grow in the world of nature and without a kernel would have no end and purpose. The *Sharīʻah* without the *Ṭarīqah* would be like a body without a soul, and the *Ṭarīqah* without the *Sharīʻah* would be devoid of an external support and simply could not subsist and manifest itself in this world. For the totality of the tradition the one like the other is absolutely necessary.

Many of the sayings of Sufi masters which on the surface seem to break or negate the *Sharīʻah* must be understood in the background of the conditions that prevailed and the audience to whom they were addressed. If a Hafez wrote that one should throw away his prayer mat or an Ibn ʻArabī wrote that his heart was the temple of idol-worshippers it does not mean that these masters were negating the Divine Law. Actually they were addressing an audience for whom the practice of the *Sharīʻah* was taken for granted and they were inviting men to transcend the world of forms by penetrating into the inner meaning of the *Sharīʻah*. There is a world of difference between a community where everyone practices the Divine Law and one where no one does so.

Today many want to transcend the world of forms without possessing the forms. They want to burn the scrolls, to use a Buddhist term, without having the scrolls. But man cannot throw away that which he does not possess. The Sufis who were inviting men to throw away the external forms were addressing persons who already possessed these forms. There was no danger of men falling below forms; the *Sharīʻah* was always present to prevent such a danger. Today they are many who live without a religious form and mistake the transcending of forms from above with a falling below the forms. The *Ṭarīqah* cannot be reached save through the *Sharī'ah* and the apparent negation of the Path is not of the *Sharī'ah* itself but the limiting of the Truth to external forms alone. Nothing is further from the intention of the Sufis than to break the *Sharī'ah* and to introduce a kind of individualism and revolt against religious forms which some modernists would like to carry out in the name of Sufism. The freedom which the *Ṭarīqah* provides through the acceptance and subsequent transcending of the forms of the Divine Law is the antipode of the quantitative 'freedom' of rejecting the Divine Law altogether. One resembles the other only in the sense that Satan is the ape of God. Only a simple soul or one who does not want to understand can mistake one freedom for the other. One cannot reject an exotericism in the name of an esotericism which one does not possess. The tree is judged by its fruit and no better proof is needed of the futility of such an attempt than the bitter fruit that it has borne.

No better proof is needed of the inner connection between the *Ṭarīqah* and the *Sharī'ah* than the fact that in many regions of the world Islam spread through Ṣufism. In certain sections of India, in Southeast Asia and in much of Africa, Islam first spread through the personal example of Sufi masters and the establishment of a Sufi order. Only afterwards did the *Sharī'ah* spread and Islam become widely accepted. Had Sufism been an alien intrusion into Islam, as many orientalists would like us to believe, how could it serve as a spearhead for the spread of the *Sharī'ah*? It is the inner link between the Law and the Way that has made possible the spread of Islam in many areas through the Sufi masters and saints who have provided a living example of Islamic spirituality.

The role of the *Ṭarīqah* as the inner dimension of the *Sharī'ah* has been even testified to by some of the authorities and founders of the schools of Law who have emphasized its importance in purifying Muslim ethics. For example it is recorded of Imam Mālik to have said, 'He who learns jurisprudence and neglects Sufism becomes a reprobate; he who learns Sufism and neglects jurisprudence becomes an apostate; and he who combines both attains the realization of the Truth.'

(من تفقه و لم يتصوف فقدتفسق، ومن تصوف و لم يتفقه فقد تزندق، ومن جمع بينهما فقدتحقق).

Also Imam al-Shāfi'ī has said, 'Three things are dear to me from your world; giving up of pretence; tempering of the personality with kindness; and following the path of the Sufis.'

(حبب الى من دنياكم ثلاث: ترك التكلف، وعشرة الخلق بالتلطف، والاقتداء بطريق اهل التصوف).

Not only an al-Ghazzālī who was a doctor of law, theologian and Sufi calls the Path followed by the Sufi the best of all paths

(ان سيرتهم احسن السير وطريقتهم اصوب الطرق)

but even an Ash'arite theologian like Fakhr al-Dīn al-Rāzī who himself was not a Sufi calls the followers of the *Ṭarīqah* those who are occupied with meditation and purification of their souls by bringing about its catharsis from material entanglements. He calls them the best group among men.

(المتصوفة قوم يشتغلون بالفكر وتجرد النفس عن العلائق الجسمانية . . . وهؤلاء هم خير فرق آدميين).

The same could be said of Shi'ite sources with even greater emphasis because the sayings of the Imams, especially 'Alī, which are one of the foundations of Shi'ite Law are also the basis of the Spiritual Path. 'Alī as the representative of esotericism in Islam is after the Prophet the direct source of the *Ṭarīqah* in both Shi'ite and Sunni Islam.

As far as the situation of the *Ṭarīqah vis-à-vis* Shi'ism and Sunnism is concerned, it is a complex relationship which cannot be fully explained in just a few words. As a first step in clarifying this relationship it can be said that there are Sunnis who follow *Taṣawwuf*, that is, belong to a *Ṭarīqah*, and there are those who follow only the *Sharī'ah*. Likewise, there are Shi'ites who follow only the Law and those who belong to a *Ṭarīqah*. Therefore, it can be said that the unity of Sufism or the *Ṭarīqah* transcends the division between Sunnism and Shi'ism which can be said to constitute together the circumference of the circle whose radii symbolize the Path. The *Ṭarīqah* exists in both the Shi'ite and Sunni worlds and is adapted in each case to the environment in which it flourishes.

But the relation is made more complex by the fact that the first Shi'ite Imam, 'Alī, is the esoteric authority himself and Shi'ite doctrine and theology incorporate, even in the formal sphere, definitely esoteric elements. Shi'ism itself contains esoteric teachings although it cannot be identified with Islamic esotericism or gnosis as such because it has its own form of the *Sharī'ah* and exoteric aspect. Therefore, regarding this very delicate and complex situation it can be said that on the one hand the *Ṭarīqah* or Sufism exists within both Sunnism and Shi'ism while on the other hand Shi'ism as a whole is a more esoteric interpretation of the Islamic revelation and contains in its teaching elements akin to those of Sufism.

As far as the final result is concerned the total structure of Islam remains unchanged; in both segments of the community, the Sunni and the Shi'ite, the Law and the Way, or the *Sharī'ah* and the *Ṭarīqah*, are present. It can even be said that if Shi'ism is the 'Islam of 'Alī', the grace or *barakah* of 'Alī is present in the Sunni world in the Sufi orders as well as the craft guilds which have been traditionally linked to the orders. The teachings of 'Alī and the other Imams which form, after the Quran and prophetic *Ḥadīth*, the foundation of Shi'ism are also present in Sufism as it exists in the Sunni world. But these teachings are present in Sufism in the Sunni world, not as those of the Shi'ite Imams but as teachings of representatives of Islamic esotericism as such. It cannot be said that Shi'ism is the origin of Sufism. But it can be said that in as much as 'Alī stands at the origin of Shi'ism, and is at the same time the outstanding representative of Islamic esotericism, the sources of Shi'ism and Sufism are in this respect the same and they have many elements in common. It must not, however, be forgotten that Shi'ism is not Islamic gnosis alone but a total orthodox interpretation of Islam which is meant for a human collectivity, and possesses, like Sunnism, both the *Sharī'ah* and the *Ṭarīqah*.

Very few Western scholars of Islam have realized that the roots of the *Ṭarīqah* lie in the Quran. Many years ago Massignon wrote that it is enough to read the Quran several times to realize that Sufism or the *Ṭarīqah* issues forth from it. Margoliouth also admitted to the Quranic origin of Sufism and of course Corbin, who has another point of view from that of most orientalists and who performs his research on Islam with a sense of personal participation, has confirmed this essential point many times. But the vast majority of Western authors, perhaps because they do not want to admit to the presence of a real spiritual dimension in Islam, have come up with all kinds of theories to explain the origin of Sufism, theories which actually all deal with the outward expressions of Sufism and not with the thing itself.

There are a number of theories about the origin of Sufism which seem to become fashionable in a cyclic manner, each coming to the fore for a while only to be discredited, fall into disrespect and then be resuscitated anew. Sufism has been said to have originated as a result of the influence of Neoplatonism, Christian monasticism, 'the Aryan reaction to a Semitic religion', Zoroastrianism and Manichaeaism, Hinduism, Buddhism and practically every other conceivable source. In each case some formal resemblance or perhaps even historical borrowing of a particular method or expression has been paraded around as new proof for the non-Islamic origin of Sufism. But almost always what has existed behind all these arguments has been the *a priori* assumption that Islam is not a Divine revelation and therefore cannot possibly have a genuine spiritual dimension of its own. There is also the age old belief in the West that Islam is just a simple and crude 'religion of the sword' which has moulded a social order by force, so that everything of a contemplative or metaphysical nature in it must have been borrowed externally.

What is overlooked by all proponents of the external origin of the *Ṭarīqah* is the actual nature of a spiritual path. A spiritual path is one through which man is able to transcend his own human limitations and approach the Divine. Therefore, the path itself cannot be man made. For man to try to transcend human nature by something devised by man himself is logically absurd. Anyone who accepts the reality of the spiritual life must accept the fact that the spiritual way must contain within itself a grace which is not man made, that it must ultimately be a path which God has ordained and placed before man to follow.

This basic truth can be applied to Sufism as well. Either the *Ṭarīqah* in Islam is a spiritual path which can produce sanctity, whose fruit bears testimony to its Divine origin through the spiritual fragrance that it carries; or it is borrowed from outside of Islam, that is, it is borrowed and devised by men and is therefore actually man made in which case it is not a spiritual path at all and there is no use talking about it as such. If, however, it can produce saints and does possess spiritual efficacy then that grace or *barakah* which makes spiritual transformation possible must be of Divine origin and, moreover, must come from the source of the Islamic revelation itself. It must be the 'Muḥammadan grace' (*al-barakat al-muḥammadīyah*), for surely a Christian or Buddhist grace could not produce a Muslim saint who is the epitome of the religious genius of Islam any more than the 'Muḥammadan grace' could produce a Buddhist or Christian saint. In both cases, however, the grace of another traditional form would be, in exceptional circumstances, an aid towards the realization of the spiritual goal.

For those who deny the authenticity of all spiritual life such arguments may not be pertinent, but surely one cannot affirm the authenticity of, let us say, Christian spirituality and negate that of Islam by appealing to purely historical arguments. In each tradition the spiritual tree must have its roots in the origins of that tradition. Every Christian would consider as absurd the assertion that the spirituality of St. Augustine is Greek on account of his knowledge of Platonism and Neoplatonism since he knows that St. Augustine became a saint not through reading books of the ancient philosophers but through the grace of Christ. The Greek sages like Plato and Plotinus provided for him a suitable language to express a truth which was Christian.

Some, however, do not realize that it is just as absurd to consider the spirituality of a Ḥallāj or Ibn 'Arabī or Rūmī non-Islamic because they may have spoken of a love that resembles the teachings of Christianity or used a certain doctrinal formulation borrowed from Neoplatonism or Hermeticism. What made these men saints was not this or that idea which such and such a Greek or Christian sage may have expressed but the 'Muḥammadan *barakah*', that real 'Divine presence' which the methods and techniques of Sufism provide. They are fruits of the spiritual tree of Islam and no tree can give fruit unless its roots are sunk in the soil that nourishes it. In the case of the spiritual tree the 'soil' must be the Divine revelation and the roots must be that direct bond which links each spiritual manifestation in a religious tradition to its origin.

To consider a somewhat different case, everyone knows that Sufism was influential in certain medieval Bhakti movements in India and some of the Hindu saints even composed mystical poetry based on Persian Sufi poems. But if these men were really saints and holy men, when they sat down and invoked 'Rama' or some other Divine Name, it must have been the grace issuing from the Hindu tradition that was present and displayed its efficacy by turning them into holy men and saints who are considered by the Hindus as the incarnation of the spiritual genius of Hinduism. It is not Sufi poetry that turned them into saints but the living presence of a spiritual current from Hinduism itself, although in the case of medieval India where two great religious traditions lived side by side a person 'was touched' sometimes by the grace of a spiritual figure from the other tradition. Yet, here again such an experience only affirms that each tradition possessed its own spiritual norm which became fully displayed in its great saints.

If so much space has been devoted to the refutation of the common orientalists' view of the origin of Sufism it is because such a view distorts the vision of the whole structure of Islam and makes impossible the true appreciation of Sufism. Once Sufism is made to be a foreign borrowing then Islam itself becomes, in foreign eyes, solely a socio-political system, which no longer appeals to the deepest spiritual urge of man. The reason for the relative neglect of the study of Islam in the field of comparative religion today is precisely because its more contemplative aspects are neglected and often dismissed as not genuine. Also, Sufism itself cannot be appreciated in its true light and taken seriously until it is realized that the *Ṭarīqah*, or the esoteric dimension of Islam, has its roots in the Quran, and like all aspects of Islamic orthodoxy is based on the twin sources of the Quran and *Ḥadīth*.

Before turning to an examination of how the *Ṭarīqah* is grounded in the Quran it is of some importance to specify the meaning of the names given to those who follow the spiritual Way. As the *Ṭarīqah* itself means the Way so does Sufism or *Taṣawwuf* in Arabic denote that Divine Wisdom (*al-ḥikmat al-ilāhīyah*) which is preserved and propagated within the *Ṭarīqah*. Whatever the etymological origin of *Taṣawwuf* may have been—whether it is derived from *ṣūf* (wool), which the early Sufis wore, or *ṣafā'* (purity), which they tried to realize, or many other words which have been discussed in medieval and modern sources—its metaphysical significance is precisely

'Divine Wisdom'. In fact in the science of numerical symbolism (*al-jafr*) connected with the Arabic alphabet, *taṣawwuf* is numerically equivalent to 'Divine Wisdom'. The Sufis themselves consider it too central and sublime a term to have been derived etymologically from any other word.

He who participates in *Tasawwuf* is called *faqīr*, or poor, according to the Quranic verse: 'And Allah is the Rich, and ye are the poor' (XLVII, 38)

(والله الغنى وانتم الفقراء)

poor being understood in the sense of the words of Christ 'Blessed are the poor in spirit'. The *faqīr* seeks to realize the 'Muḥammadan poverty' (*al-faqr al-muḥammadī*), that is, to realize that he has nothing, all comes from Allah; to realize that metaphysically he is nothing; Allah is the one and only Being. In the languages of the Islamic peoples a *faqīr* is never called a Sufi. That would be impolite, for a Sufi is one who has already realized the end of the Path, the Supreme Union. Rather, he is called a *mutaṣawwif*, he who participates in *Taṣawwuf*. And then there are always those who only play with the teachings of Sufism without really participating in them. Such a person is called the *mustaṣwif* (he who pretends to Sufism) who, as a Sufi master has said, is like a fly flying around sweets.

Of course the Sufis are also called by many other names such as the 'people of the Way' (*ahl al-ṭariqah*), the 'people who learn through allusion' (*ahl al-ishārah*), the 'people of the heart' (*ahl-i dil* in Persian) and many other appellations, each of which corresponds to a certain aspect of the reality of Sufism. The *faqīr* is also called in Persian *darvīsh* (from which comes the English word dervish) and this term is used in general in other languages of the eastern lands of Islam. He is also called the *murīd* (he who seeks or wills to follow the *Ṭarīqah*). The spiritual master, whose presence is absolutely essential as the guide on the perilous journey towards spiritual realization, is also known by several names such as *shaikh* (elder or master), *murshid* (he who guides), *murād* (he who is sought) and in Persian *pīr* (meaning, again, elder). These are all technical terms belonging to the vocabulary of Sufism each of which denotes an aspect of the spiritual life.

If we have avoided calling Sufism 'Islamic mysticism' it is

only because of the 'passive' and 'anti-intellectual' colour that this word has come to possess in most contemporary European languages as a result of several centuries of struggle between Christianity and rationalism. Sufism is an active participation in a spiritual path and is intellectual in the real meaning of this word. Contemplation in Sufism is the highest form of activity and in fact Sufism has always integrated the active and contemplative lives. That is why many Sufis have been teachers and scholars, artists and scientists, and even statesmen and soldiers. If we were to use mysticism in its original sense as that which is concerned with the 'Divine Mysteries' and consider as mystics men like St. Augustine, Eckhart or Gregory of Palamas then we could certainly call Sufism Islamic mysticism and the Sufis mystics. But then the current colour given to this word must be removed and its original meaning re-instated. In any case it must be remembered that Sufism is to follow a spiritual path based on the Quran and prophetic practice actively with the aim of gaining that illuminative knowledge (*al-'irfān*) which is the ultimate goal of the Way. In fact Sufism is cometimes called *'irfān* especially when its doctrinal aspect is under consideration.

The *Ṭarīqah* has its roots in the Quran and prophetic *Ḥadīth* in both doctrine and practice. Doctrinally the Sufi seeks to realize the meaning of the *Shahādah, Lā ilāha ill'Allāh*, and practically he seeks to emulate the life of the Prophet who is the prototype of Islamic spirituality and who realized the unity or *tawḥīd* implied by the *Shahādah* in its fullness. The Sufi begins by asking what does it really mean to say *Lā ilāha ill'Allāh*. He discovers the answer by living a life in conformity with the example set by the Prophet who had fully realized the import of this testament. *Taṣawwuf* begins with the quest after the ultimate meaning of the fundamental doctrinal formulation of Islam.

The realization of Unity as contained in the *Shahādah* is achieved by the Sufi precisely through basing his life on that of the Prophet who is the prototype of the spiritual life in Islam. No group of people in Islamic society have ever sought to emulate the life of the Prophet with the same rigour and intensity as the Sufis. Not only do the Sufis seek to live in their daily life according to prophetic *Sunnah*, but they also walk upon the Path in quest of the spiritual experience whose perfect norm is the nocturnal ascent (*al-mi'rāj*) of the Prophet.

On a certain night, while in Mecca, the Prophet was taken to Jerusalem and there ascended through the heavens, or the multiple states of being which the concentric heavens of traditional astronomy symbolize, to the Divine Presence itself. Accompanied by the archangel Gabriel, who was his guide, the Prophet journeyed through all the worlds until he reached a limit when the archangel refused to pass any further saying that if he were to proceed his wings would 'burn', implying that the final stage of the journey was beyond even the highest degree of manifestation which is that of the archangel. Moreover, the Prophet accomplished this journey not only 'mentally' or 'spiritually' but also 'physically'. This implies that the journey symbolizes the integration of his whole being including the body just as resurrection is also bodily and, in another context, the Quran was received in the body of the Prophet.

This *mi'rāj* or ascension is the prototype of the spiritual journey of the Sufi who can however hope to accomplish it in this life only spiritually and not with his total being including the body. To journey from one stage of being to another, ascending the ladder of the universal hierarchy of being to the Divine Presence, that is the goal of the *Ṭarīqah*, and it is based on the example of the Prophet. Many a Sufi has written of the spiritual significance of the nocturnal ascent such as the great Persian Sufi poet Sanā'ī whose *Mi'rāj-nāmah* (*Treatise of the Nocturnal Ascent*) along with certain other Sufi sources served as an inspiration for Dante. The Florentine poet in his *Divine Comedy* employs the symbolism of journeying through the cosmos to depict the ascension of the soul towards God, describing a cosmos which, however, is Christian although the model Dante used came from Islamic sources.

Not only is the practice of the Sufis or people of the *Ṭarīqah* based on the life and example of the Prophet but its foundation lies in the Quran itself which speaks of *islām* (*Surrender*), *īmān* (faith), and *iḥsān* (virtue). Also it was once asked of the Prophet what is religion (*al-dīn*). He answered that it is comprised of the three elements of *islām*, *īmān* and *iḥsān*, the first of which has given its name to the religious tradition itself. Everyone who accepts this religion and surrenders himself to the Divine Will is called ***muslim*** but not every Muslim is a ***mu'min*** or calls himself so. ***Īmān*** is a stronger degree of participation in the religion implying intense faith and attachment to God. As for ***iḥsān*** it is an even more profound penetration into the heart of the revelation through the possession of that 'virtue' which is not given to all. It is, in fact, that reality which the *Ṭarīqah* contains and seeks to inculcate in those who follow it.

Īmān is essentially faith in Divine Unity and ***islām*** submission to the Divine Will. *Iḥsān* operates upon these two fundamental elements of the religion and transforms them into what is known as *Taṣawwuf*. In fact, the Sufi masters have over the ages defined Sufism by the well-known *Ḥadīth* of the Prophet who when asked about the definition of *iḥsān* said: '*Iḥsān* is to adore Allah as though thou didst see him, and if thou doest not see him he nonetheless sees thee.'

(الاحسان ان تعبد الله كانك تراه فان لم تكن تراه فانه يراك)

This definition is essentially also that of Sufism.

What the *Ṭarīqah* teaches is precisely to worship God with the awareness that we are in His proximity and therefore 'see' Him or that He is always watching us and we are always standing before Him. It seeks to bring the disciple into the awareness that he is always living in the Divine Presence. *Taṣawwuf* applies this virtue or ***iḥsān*** to both ***īmān*** and ***islām***. ***Īmān***, when transformed by ***iḥsān***, becomes that illuminative knowledge that unites, that gnosis (*'irfān* or *ma'rifah*) which penetrates and transforms man. *Islām* when seen in the light of ***iḥsān*** becomes extinction in the Divine (*al-fanā'*), the realization that before God we are nothing and He is everything.

Many a Sufi master has identified *iḥsān* with sincerity (*ikhlāṣ*) in religion. To possess this sincerity is to make one's religion central and to try to penetrate into its inner meaning with all one's being. Applied to the first *Shahādah*, *Lā ilāha ill'Allāh*, it becomes the means of attaining knowledge. All of metaphysics, all of the doctrine of the *Ṭarīqah*, is contained in the *Shahādah* and can be understood when seen with the eye of *ikhlāṣ* or *iḥsān*. Applied to the second *Shahādah*, *Muḥammadun rasūl Allāh*, it provides the spiritual virtues and attitudes which the *Ṭarīqah* seeks to inculcate and which alone make the realization of the Truth possible. The *Ṭarīqah*, therefore, contains two basic elements and two kinds of teachings, a doctrine about the nature of reality or metaphysics and a spiritual instruction about the stages of the Path. Every Sufi text, in fact, is either the exposition of metaphysics and cosmology or the explanation of the spiritual virtues whose attainment leads man towards sanctity and the realization of his 'God-like' nature.

Sufism, like every true spiritual way, is thus based on a doctrine and a method, on discernment and union. The doctrine teaches essentially that only God is absolutely Real; everything else is relative. It is a means of discernment. The method teaches the means of uniting with the Real. It contains the means of union. Both the doctrine and the method are essential and both issue from the two *Shahādahs* as seen in the light of that 'sincerity' or 'virtue' that belongs to the *Ṭarīqah.*

It can also be said that from another point of view the Way contains three elements all of which are necessary: doctrine, spiritual virtues and a spiritual alchemy or means of transforming the soul and enabling it to realize the virtues and penetrate the doctrine. The *Ṭarīqah* contains all these elements which derive from the source of the revelation. Not only the doctrine and the virtues come from the Quran and prophetic *Sunnah,* but also that grace which is indispensable for the realization of the spiritual alchemy issues from the Prophet. It is that 'Muhammadan grace' (*al-barakat al-muḥammadīyah*), contained in the *Ṭarīqah,* that makes the spiritual journey possible. Together with the doctrine and the spiritual virtues they constitute the spiritual Way in Islam whose end is the realization of 'Muḥammadan poverty'.

The doctrine should not, however, be mistaken for philosophy as this term is usually used in Western languages although in the eastern lands of Islam philosophy, when connected with the name of such sages as Suhrawardī and Mullā Ṣadrā, is essentially wisdom or *ḥikmah* and therefore closely related to Sufi doctrine. The doctrine connected with the *Ṭarīqah* is not philosophy in the sense that it does not seek to encompass reality in a rationalistic system. Rather, in its external formulation, it is theory (*theoria*) in the original Greek sense of vision and as it is still understood in Hesychasm in the West. It is an intellectual vision of the Truth, a vision of the anatomy of the Universe and man's situation in it as well as of the Divine Attributes and

Qualities. And it is a vision made possible through the instrument of the intellect.

The tragedy of modern Western philosophy lies, from the Muslim point of view, in confusing intellect and reason. The intellect to which the Sufi doctrine appeals and through which it is understood is that instrument of knowledge which perceives directly. It is not reason which is, at best, its mental image. *Intellectus* is not *ratio*. The latter can create and understand philosophy in the usual meaning of the word; only the former can understand metaphysics in its true sense which lies at the heart of the doctrine. To comprehend the doctrine is therefore not just to try to conform ideas to a logical pattern. Nor is it to play with ideas and seek to perform any kind of mental acrobatics. It is a contemplative vision of the nature of things made possible through intellection. The doctrine or metaphysics would be the easiest thing to teach if all men could understand as easily as they can reason. But in fact it is most difficult to explain precisely because only a few are capable of intellection. That is why even within the *Ṭarīqah* only a small number are capable of fully comprehending the doctrine.

Doctrine is in a sense the beginning and end of the Path. It comes at the beginning as a knowledge that is 'theoretical' and at the end as one that is realized and lived. Between the two there is a world of difference. Every doctrinal work of Sufism is like a key with which a particular door is opened and through which the traveller must pass until finally, at the end of the road, he realizes in his being the doctrine that he knew 'theoretically' at the beginning. There are those who belittle doctrine in the name of experience. But doctrine is absolutely essential especially at the beginning of the Path when man is lost in the maze of distracting thoughts, and especially in modern times when the confusion in the mental plane makes the possession of a clear vision of the nature of things indispensable. The doctrine at the beginning is like the map of a mountain to be climbed. At the end it is the intimate knowledge of the mountain gained through the actual experience of having climbed it.

Also in the same way that different descriptions can be given of a mountain depending on the angle from which it is being viewed, doctrine is often expressed in terms that may seem contradictory in certain external aspects. But the subject of all the descriptions is the mountain and the content of all the expressions of doctrine is the Truth which each formulation expresses from a certain point of view. In metaphysical doctrines there is no innate opposition, as in schools of philosophy, but complementary forms that reveal the same essence.

All doctrine, as already stated, is essentially the distinction between the Real and the apparent, the Absolute and relative, or substance and accidents. Its cardinal teaching is that only Allah is absolutely Real and consequently this world in which man lives is contingent. Between God, who transcends Being and whose first determination is Pure Being, and this world, which is farthest away from It, there are located a number of other worlds each standing hierarchically above the other in the scale of universal existence. Together they comprise the multiple states of being, which all receive their being from God, while before Him they are literally nothing. Man thus stands before this vast number of worlds above him, and beyond them before the Divine Presence Itself which, although completely transcendent with respect to all domains of the Universe, is closer to man than his jugular vein.

The central doctrine concerning the ultimate nature of reality has usually been called *waḥdat al-wujūd* or the (transcendent) unity of Being. This cardinal doctrine, which is not pantheism, not pan-entheism nor natural mysticism as Western orientalists have called it, is the direct consequence of the *Shahādah*. It asserts that there cannot be two completely independent orders of reality or being which would be sheer polytheism or *shirk*. Therefore, to the extent that anything has being it cannot be other than the Absolute Being. The *Shahādah* in fact begins with the *lā*, or negation, in order to absolve Reality of all otherness and multiplicity. The relation between God and the order of existence is not just a logical one in which if one thing is equal to another the other is equal to the first. Through that mystery that lies in the heart of creation itself, everything is, in essence, identified with God while God infinitely transcends everything. To understand this doctrine intellectually is to possess contemplative intelligence; to realize it fully is to be a saint who alone sees 'God everywhere'.

Next in importance to the Unity of Being is the doctrine of Universal Man (*al-insān al-kāmil*), which is its concomitant.

Man, as envisaged in Sufism is not just 'the rational animal' as usually understood, but a being who possesses in himself all the multiple states of being, although the vast majority of men are not aware of the amplitude of their nature and the possibilities that they bear within themselves. Only the saint realizes the totality of the nature of universal man and thereby becomes the perfect mirror in which God contemplates Himself. God created the world so that He might be known according to the sacred *Ḥadīth* 'I was a hidden treasure; I wanted to be known, therefore I created the world.'

(كنت كنزاً مخفياً واحببت ان اعرف فخلقت العالم).

The Universal Man is the mirror in which the Divine Names and Qualities are fully reflected and through which the purpose of creation itself is fulfilled.

The multiple states of being which man bears within himself make him a counterpart of the Universe, and for this reason one is called the microcosm and the other the macrocosm. Both reflect in their being and symbolism the Metacosm which is their source. This metaphysical reality is prefigured in medieval cosmology in which, in the Universe, the earth stands at the centre surrounded by concentric spheres each of which symbolizes a degree of being which approaches God in an ascending order. At the highest sphere stands the First Intellect or Spirit (*Rūḥ*), above which there is the Divine Presence Itself. Within man the order is present but reversed in the sense that the 'earth', or most material part of him, is the body, which is also the most outward shell. Within lies the psyche, which in turn surrounds the inner soul, leading finally to the Spirit which reigns in the innermost centre or heart of man. The heart is in fact called the 'Throne of the Compassionate' (*'arsh al-raḥmān*), like the highest heaven. Man is constituted in such a way that he occupies a central position in the world and is able to realize the Truth contained in the doctrine by realizing the totality of the nature of Universal Man. Such a potentiality is always present and can become actualized if a person undergoes the spiritual discipline of the *Ṭarīqah* and realizes the spiritual virtues which are human ways of being in conformity with the Truth and realizing the Truth in oneself.

The spiritual virtues are, alongside with the doctrine, the

indispensable element of the *Ṭarīqah*. They are the means through which man can attain the saintly life. The virtues in the *Ṭarīqah* are not, of course, the over-sentimentalized virtues which one finds in many religious circles in the West today and which have driven many an intelligent person away from religion. They are rather a manner of 'being' the Truth, as the doctrine is a manner of knowing It. That is why without the spiritual virtues it is not possible to realize the Truth in one's life and in the substance of one's soul. Man is not just a mind that thinks, but a creature that exists. Therefore both his knowledge and his existence have to be transformed. The virtues are not man-made moral attitudes; they are 'manners of being', which transform man's existence in conformity with his inner nature. They are apophatic virtues which must be realized if man is to bear the fragrance of spirituality.

The cardinal spiritual virtues in *Taṣawwuf*, which in fact characterize spiritual life as such, are humility, charity and truthfulness, which are in essence the same virtues that characterize the Prophet. Humility in Islam does not mean a sentimental attitude of meekness which hides the pride of the ego. Nor does it mean the hatred of intelligence, as is so often seen in certain trends of Western religious thought today. There are those who hate intelligence in the name of humility and even consider gnosis as pride as if the gnostic were not called 'He who knows *by* God' (*al-'ārif bi'llāh*), therefore one who knows God through God Himself and not through purely human knowledge. To hate the intelligence is to hate the most precious gift that God has given to man. It is in Christian terms to sin against the Holy Ghost, and it is the attitude farthest removed from the real meaning of humility in *Taṣawwuf*.

Humility as a spiritual virtue means to realize that God is everything and we are nothing, and on another level that our neighbour—which means not only man but every creature in the Universe—can teach us something through possessing a perfection which we do not have. It means that *vis-à-vis* God we realize our impotence and see the triviality of the human before the Divine. With regard to our neighbour it means to live in constant awareness that, however perfect we might be, others have certain perfections that we lack, and therefore we should be humble before them. Humility is against that pride which blinds the ego to its own limitations so that it seeks to assert itself, not only before man, but even before God, forgetting its own pettiness and its utter reliance upon the Divine before whose majesty man is reduced to nothingness.

As for charity, as a spiritual virtue it is not that quantitative and materialistic charity that is so prevalent today. Many want to be charitable towards men without the concomitant attitude of reverence towards God. Thus man who is the subject of charity becomes a two-legged animal whose physical needs alone are considered and his deeper needs, such as beauty and love, become ignored or are relegated to the category of luxuries. There is no common measure between spiritual charity, the charity of the saints, and the humanistic and materialistic charity that ultimately reduces man to an animal and which provides him with food and clothing while depriving him of shelter in the real meaning of that word. It teaches him how to walk, while depriving him of his eyesight, which alone could tell him where to go.

Islam considers the whole of man and believes that one should either concern himself with the whole man or not bother to concern himself with him at all. A charity which concerns itself only with the animal needs of man ends in doing more harm to him than no charity at all. The charity which is cultivated in the *Ṭarīqah* is, in fact, concerned not only with the external act and the moral attitude connected with it but also, and most of all, with a state of being. Man must be charitable not because of any altruistic motives but because ultimately he is himself in need of it, because it is in the nature of things.

The carnal soul of man or his separative existence weighs heavily upon his shoulders. Only the saint is able to offer his soul in sacrifice to God. And in giving himself to God the saint performs the greatest act of charity even if he were not to feed a single mouth. His presence in society alone is the highest charity for the human collectivity. As for other men, it is the act of performing a good deed that lifts the heavy burden of their carnal soul (*al-nafs al-ammārah*). In giving himself to others man is himself uplifted. However, this act of charity has a spiritual efficacy only when it is done with the awareness that all good comes from God and that without Him no act can be truly charitable. One must realize that the Universe is ultimately one and that man finds in all things his own inner self. Man must realize that in giving himself to God he gives himself to his neighbour and in offering himself to others he is offering his soul to God. Spiritual charity implies a melting of the solidified soul so that it flows and expands to embrace all things. If humility is the death of something in the soul or its contraction (*inqibāḍ*), so is spiritual charity an expansion (*inbisāṭ*), through which man realizes his oneness with all beings, including not only men but all creatures.

The third virtue, sincerity (*ikhlāṣ*), or truthfulness (*ṣidq*), is the culmination of the other two and is based upon them. This virtue, which in general characterizes Islam itself, means to see things as they are, in their true nature which does not veil but reveals the Divine. It means to see God everywhere. There is a *Ḥadīth* according to which the Prophet saw nothing without seeing God before it, in it and after it. This is perfect sincerity. Truthfulness or sincerity is, therefore, the virtue by means of which man realizes unity or *tawḥīd* and lives in the constant presence of God. By acquiring this virtue he actually realizes as experience the doctrine which he comes to know 'theoretically' at the beginning of the Path.

The operational technique of the *Ṭarīqah* for the realization of the virtues and the doctrine is based on the Islamic conception of man which has been outlined already. God created man 'upon His own image (*ṣūrah*)' by virtue of which he has this theomorphic nature that so many men ignore although it exists within them. As a result of possessing this nature man is given certain qualities which, in their fullness, belong to God alone. God is Alive (*ḥayy*), therefore man is given life. He has Will, therefore man is given free will, and He has the Quality of Speech or the Word (*kalimah*), so that man is given the power of speech. The *Ṭarīqah* bases its techniques on those very Divine Qualities which are reflected in man but which, in their perfection, belong to God alone.

The Quran asserts that God created the world through His Word. 'But His command, when He intendeth a thing, is only that He saith unto it: Be! and it is.' (XXXVI, 81).

(انما امره اذا اراد شيئاً ان يقول له كن فيكون)

The Divine Word therefore performs two functions; it creates and it transmits the Truth. The world was created by the Word and all revelation comes from the Word or Logos. It is also through the Word and the power of speech that man returns to God.

Human speech has the ability to express the Truth and of transforming man, thus 'reversing' the process of creation from the point of view of its being separation and elongation from the Divine. According to Sufism, human speech has essentially two functions: to give a discourse on some aspect of Truth or to pray, the first corresponding to the function of the Divine Word as bringer of revelation and the second to its power of creating the world. In fact the very substance of world is 'prayer'; existence is 'prayer'. The world was brought into being by the 'Breath of the Compassionate' (*nafas al-raḥmān*) so that its ultimate substance is the 'Breath', which, in the human state is connected intimately with speech.

The primary spiritual technique of Sufism is therefore prayer through which man returns to God, prayer in its most universal sense as it becomes ultimately unified with the rhythm of life itself. Prayer is essentially the remembrance of God (*dhikr*). It is in fact extremely significant that in Arabic the word *dhikr*, which is the basic technique of Sufism, means both invocation and remembrance. Invocation of a Divine Name, which is the most universal form of prayer and exists also in other traditions, brings about also the remembrance of God and an awakening from the dream of forgetfulness. Prayer in this sense makes and transforms man until he himself becomes 'prayer', identified with the *dhikr* which becomes his real nature and in which he discovers who he really is.

There are many verses of the Quran instructing men to invoke the Name of God, which in a spiritual sense can, however be practiced only under the guidance of a master and through the aid of the discipline offered by the *Ṭarīqah*. Man is, in fact, guaranteed in the Quran that this is the means to approach God, for the Quran asserts: 'Therefore remember Me, I will remember you.' (II, 152)

(فاذكروني اذكركم).

Likewise, there are many *Ḥadīths* concerning the importance of invocation of which the following *Ḥadīth qudsī*, is an example: 'He who mentions me in himself I will mention him in Myself, and he who mentions Me in an assembly, him I will mention in an assembly better than his [i.e., in Heaven].'

These Quranic and prophetic sources are the traditional basis of the Sufi technique of *dhikr* in all its forms. Through the practice of invocation man realizes the spiritual virtues and the doctrine and ultimately awakens from all dreaming, realizing his true nature and real self above and beyond all domains of contingency and limitation. If before he was man (*insān*) because of his *nisyān* or forgetfulness, now he becomes *insān* in the true sense because of his *uns* or familiarity with the Divine.

The means of dispensing the spiritual method is contained in Islam within the Sufi orders or *Ṭuruq*. These orders have preserved the means of spiritual realization from one generation to the next. In fact the efficacy of the method is guaranteed only by that regularity of the initiatic chain (*silsilah*) which goes back to the Prophet himself and transmits his particular *barakah* from generation to generation. The esoteric instructions of the Prophet were given to only a few companions who are the first Sufis. Only later, in the third century, did these groups become formalized into orders identified with a particular master. In conformity with the nature of Islamic revelation the orders of the *Ṭarīqah* and the schools of the *Sharī'ah* became distinct and formalized at about the same time, although both reach back to the origin of the Islamic revelation and begin with the Prophet himself.

It is the regularity of initiative transmission within the Sufi orders that permits the 'spiritual presence' or *barakah* to be ever alive and to operate the transmuting of the soul from the chaotic to the illuminated state. The methods of Sufism can, in fact, be practiced with safety only under the direction of a master and within an order. Otherwise they can cause the deepest psychic disequilibrium. The danger of a fall in mountain climbing is much greater than when one walks on flat ground and it is in climbing a mountain, both the physical and spiritual, that man needs a guide unless he has himself climbed before and has become in turn a guide for others.

The importance of the *Ṭuruq* even on the social and external plane has been so immense in Islamic history that no student of any aspect of Islam can afford to neglect it. The relation of the orders with the craft guilds, with learning, with certain orders of chivalry and with the perenial renovation of the social ethics of Muslim society are too obvious to be overlooked. But the most important role of the *Ṭarīqah* is that it is the dispenser of that method and grace that make the spiritual life possible. Rooted in the Quran and the *Sharī'ah* it is like a tree whose branches stretch outward towards heaven. Its function has always been to reveal the inner meaning of the *Sharī'ah*, to bring man to understand what it really means to be the slave (*'abd*) of God, namely to realize that He is everything and we are nothing.

The *Ṭarīqah* is based on a doctrine that is essentially a commentary upon the two *Shahādahs*, a set of spiritual virtues which are those that the Prophet possessed in their fullness, and on a method which is intimately connected with the rites of the *Sharī'ah* and carries the meaning of prayer to its universal level. Its method and outlook combine fear, love and knowledge of God all of which play a role in man's realization of his spiritual nature. The *Ṭarīqah* is the Way of sanctity in Islam and it is the *Ṭarīqah* that has produced saints over the centuries to the present day, saints who keep society together and rejuvenate its religious life by vitalizing it with the spiritual forces which have brought the religion itself into being. The perfume of Islamic spirituality is never divorced from the life of those who walk upon the Way or the *Ṭarīqah* and who realize that supreme state of spiritual perfection which is man's end and the final purpose of his existence.

Suggestions for further reading

Anawati, G. C., and Gardet, L., *La Mystique musulmane*, Paris, J. Vrin, 1961. A systematic yet brief history of Sufism and a study of the main Sufi spiritual techniques containing much of value although the point of view is that of considering Sufism as natural mysticism.

Asin Palacios, M., *El Islam cristianazado*, Madrid, Plutarco, 1931. Although based on a thesis which cannot be accepted by Muslims, this work contains a wealth of information on Sufism especially that of Andalusia written by a Spanish orientalist who has devoted many studies to the Sufis of that land.

Burckhardt, T., *An Introduction to Sufi Doctrine*, trans. D. M. Matheson, Lahore, Muhammad Ashraf, 1959. The most lucid exposition of Sufi doctrine in a European language and an indispensable introduction to any serious study of Sufism based on Western sources, written with authority and from within the Sufi tradition.

Corbin, H., *En Islam iranien*, 4 vols., Paris, Gallimard, 1971–72. A monumental work summarizing a life-time of research on Islam in Persia. The first volume contains a detailed study of Shi'ism in its esoteric and metaphysical aspects while the third volume is devoted to Sufism in its various manifestations in Persia.

—*L'Imagination créatrice dans le soufisme d'Ibn 'Arabī*, Paris, Flammarion, 1958. An analysis of certain aspects of the Sufism of Ibn 'Arabī and its influence in the East carried out with sympathy by one who accepts the spiritual originality and creativity of Sufism although his interest is essentially confined to the relation of Sufism with the Shī'ite world.

Hujwiri, *Kashf al-Maḥjūb*, trans. R. A. Nicholson, London, "E. J. W. Gibb Memorial," Luzac and Co., 1911. A fine translation of one of the earliest and most authoritative works of Sufism containing the essential Sufi teachings as they have been practised and followed over the centuries.

Ikbal Ali Shah, S., *Islamic Sufism*, London, Rider and Co., 1933. A discussion of Sufism by a contemporary Sufi although some of the references made to Western concepts and ideas are inaccurate and many misleading for a Westerner not already acquainted with Sufism.

Lings, M., *A Moslem Saint of the Twentieth Century*, London, Allen and Unwin, 1961. Also as *A Sufi Saint of the Twentieth Century*, London, Allen & Unwin, 1971; Los Angeles, University of California Press, 1972. A precious and indispensable study of a contemporary Sufi master containing both a sympathetic portrait of the saint and selections of his writings on salient features of Sufism.

Massignon, L., *La Passion d'al-Hallaj*, 2 vols., Paris, P. Geuthner, 1922. The magnum opus of the leading French orientalist who devoted a life time to the study of Sufism and displayed much sympathy and profound insight in his writings on the Sufis and especially on Ḥallāj.

—*Recueil de textes inédits concernant l'histoire de la mystique en pays d'Islam*, Paris, P. Geuthner, 1929. The pioneering European work on the history of Sufism based on close textual study and a vast knowledge of Sufi writings.

Mir Valiuddin, *The Quranic Sufism*, Delhi, Asia House, 1959. Sufism as based directly on the Quran studied sympathetically from the point of view of the Sufi tradition.

Nasr, S. H., *Science and Civilization in Islam*, Cambridge (USA), Harvard University Press, 1968; New York, New American Library (Plume Books), 1970. Besides treating the relation between Islamic science and Sufism, the final chapter contains a summary of the doctrines of Sufism.

Nasr, S. H., *Sufi Essays*, London, Allen & Unwin, 1972. A collection of essays on various aspects of Sufism and the application of the principles of Sufism to the solution of some outstanding contemporary problems.

—*Three Muslim Sages*, Cambridge, Harvard University Press, 1964. A study of the School of Illumination of Suhrawardī and the Sufism of Ibn 'Arabī and his followers.

Nicholson, R., *Studies in Islamic Mysticism*, Cambridge, University Press, 1919. The best known work of the translator of the *Mathnawī* and a leading English orientalist, containing good translations of important Sufi works and an analysis which however is too much coloured by categories of European philosophy.

Schaya, L., *La Doctrine soufique de l'Unité*, Paris, Andrien-Maisonneuve, 1962. The traditional exposition of the doctrine of Unity based mostly on the writings of the school of Ibn 'Arabī.

Schuon, F., *Dimensions of Islam*, trans. by P. Townsend, London, Allen & Unwin, 1970. Discusses with amazing penetration some of the most delicate metaphysical questions of Islamic gnosis.

—*L'Oeil du coeur*, Paris, Gallimard, 1950. An exposition of many different aspects of Sufi doctrine including cosmology and the position of Sufism in the Islamic tradition.

—*Spiritual Perspectives and Human Facts*, trans. D. M. Matheson, London, Faber and Faber, 1953. Contains a masterly comparison between Sufism and the Vedanta as well as a discussion of the spiritual virtues and their role in Sufism.

—*Understanding Islam*, London, Allen and Unwin, 1963. Chapter IV. The outstanding study of Sufism as the esoteric dimension of Islam and as rooted directly in the Quran.

Siraj ed-Din, Abu Bakr, *The Book of Certainty*, London, Rider and Co., 1952; New York, S. Weiser, 1970. A contemporary Sufi work on some of the teachings of Sufism based on the traditional symbolism of the degrees of certainty.

Trimingham, J. Spencer, *The Sufi Orders in Islam*, Oxford, Clarendon Press, 1971; New York, Oxford University Press (Galaxy Books), 1972. The most thorough study in recent years on the history and organization of the Sufi orders.

CHAPTER VI

Sunnism and Shi'ism
Twelve-Imam Shi'ism and Isma'ilism

Since every religion addresses a collectivity with varying psychological and spiritual temperaments, it must possess within itself the possibility of different interpretations. By bearing within itself, providentially, several modes of interpretation of the same truth it is able to integrate a multiplicity into unity and to create a religous civilization. In traditional Christianity one finds the Catholic and Orthodox churches, not to speak of the smaller eastern churches such as the Coptic and Maronite. And outside the Abrahamic family there is Buddhism with its two major schools of Mahayana and Theravada—and in addition the Tibetan form. Without the Mahayana, or northern school, it is doubtful whether this tradition could have become dominant in the Far East. Likewise, Hinduism which, like a vast sea, contains within itself numerous spiritual forms, is again divided into the Shaivite and Vaishnavite interpretations to suit different spiritual temperaments.

In Islam, which is a world-wide religion meant for various ethnic and racial types, there also existed from the beginning the possibility of two different perspectives. Sunnism and Shi'ism are both orthodox interpretations of the Islamic revelation contained providentially within Islam in order to enable it to integrate people of different psychological constitutions into itself. Both Sunnism and Shi'ism constitute an integral part of Islamic orthodoxy which existed from the beginning. Shi'ism is not heterodox nor is it a sect although within the world of Shi'ism there have been groups who have deviated from the main orthodoxy and are sects in the real sense.

Neither Shi'ism nor Sunnism is a late revolt against an

established orthodoxy and should therefore not be compared in any way with reform movements in Christianity or Judaism. In fact Sunnism and Shi'ism, belonging both to the total orthodoxy of Islam, do not in any way destroy its unity. The unity of a tradition is not destroyed by different applications of it but by the destruction of its principles and forms as well as its continuity. Being 'the religion of unity' Islam, in fact, displays more homogeneity and less religious diversity than other world-wide religions. Sunnism and Shi'ism are dimensions within Islam placed there not to destroy its unity but to enable a larger humanity and differing spiritual types to participate in it. Both Sunnism and Shi'ism are the assertion of the *Shahādah, Lā ilāha ill'Allāh,* expressed in different climates and with a somewhat different spiritual fragrance.

To say that Sunnism and Shi'ism were meant for different spiritual temperaments should not, however, be interpreted strictly in a racial or ethnical sense. One should not think that a particular people has always been solidly Sunni and another Shi'ite. Of course, today the Persians are nearly all Shi'ite while most Arabs and Turks are Sunnis and these ethnic divisions do have a relation with the distribution of Sunnism and Shi'ism in the Muslim world. But it must also be recalled that during the third/tenth and fourth/eleventh centuries the stronghold of Shi'ism was southern Syria and North Africa while Khurasan was the bastion of Sunnism. Such great champions of Sunni Islam as al-Ghazzālī and Fakhr al-Dīn al-Rāzī were Persians, and Ash'arite theology, which is often called 'orthodox' Sunni theology, had its early foundation and development, to a large extent, in the hands of Persians. Nevertheless, once this point is considered, it can be said with safety that the Persians were generally sympathetic to the cause of Shi'ism from the beginning and it was in this land that, after the Mongol invasion, Shi'ism became gradually more dominant until, with the Safavids, it became the state religion. Without forgetting the large number of Arab and Indo-Pakistani Shi'ites, one can also add that the Persians form the largest body of Shi'ism in the world and Shi'ite Islam has an intimate connection with the Persian soul.

In dealing with Sunnism and Shi'ism in this chapter we shall speak more about Shi'ism, accepting Sunnism as the norm and background with which it is compared. The reason for this procedure is that Sunni Islam is much better known in the external world than Shi'ism as the West has had more historical contact with Sunnism. In fact nearly every book in European languages concerning Islam studies it from Sunni sources, although, alas, usually not without distortion and prejudice. Shi'ism, and especially the Twelve-imam school, is nearly unknown in European works save for the writings of a very small number of scholars of whom the notable one is Henry Corbin. Moreover, in previous chapters most of what has been said concerns Islam in general and Sunnism in particular, so that it is natural that, in this chapter, after devoting a brief discussion to Sunnism we should turn our attention to Shi'ism whose beliefs we should seek to clarify both in themselves and in relation to Sunnism.

In order to understand the Sunni and Shi'ite perspectives it is necessary to glance at the religious history of Islam, the development of these two dimensions from their common origin and their subsequent history. From an external point of view the difference between Sunnism and Shi'ism concerns the problem of 'successor' to the Prophet as the leader of the community after his death. The two schools may thus be said to have begun as distinct entities when the Prophet finished his earthly career, because it was precisely at this moment that difference of opinion as to his successor arose. A small group believed that such a function must remain in the family of the Prophet and backed 'Alī, whom they believed to have been designated for this role by appointment (*ta'yīn*) and testament (*naṣṣ*). They became known as his 'partisans' (*shī'ah*) while the majority agreed on Abū Bakr on the assumption that the Prophet left no instruction on this matter; they gained the name of 'The People of tradition and the consensus of opinion' (*ahl al-sunnah wa'l-jamā'ah*). But more generally the Shi'ah of 'Alī, in the sense of those who backed and followed him among the companions, already existed during the Prophet's lifetime and there are several references to them in prophetic sayings. Only with the death of the Prophet did they become crystallized as a group distinct from the Sunnis.

But the question also involved the function of the person who was to succeed the Prophet, for surely such a person could not continue to possess prophetic powers. Thus Sunnism considered the 'successor' of the Prophet to be his *khalīfah* or caliph only in his capacity as the ruler of a newly founded community while the Shi'ites believed that the 'successor' must also be the 'trusted' (*waṣī*) of his esoteric knowledge and the interpreter of the religious sciences. That is why although the difference between Sunnism and Shi'ism appears to be only a political one it is, in reality, more than that. It is also theological. There is a question of both political succession and religious authority.

Some recent works of orientalists have, in fact, tried to reduce the distinction between Sunnism and Shi'ism to a sheer political one. Although this view is to a certain extent true, such a perspective leaves aside the more important religious and theological considerations involved. The question of who was to succeed the Prophet as the leader of the community was combined with two different conceptions of the qualifications of the successor and the meaning of religious authority itself. Sunni Islam considered the *khalīfah* to be a guardian of the *Sharī'ah* in the community, while Shi'ism saw in the 'successor' a spiritual function connected with the esoteric interpretation of the revelation and the inheritance of the Prophet's esoteric teachings. Thereby began the two different interpretations of that one Divine message, two interpretations which nevertheless remain within the total orthodoxy of Islam and are unified in the principles of religion (*uṣūl al-dīn*) and the religious rites, which are the means of grace for saving man and assuring him felicity in the hereafter.

As far as Sunnism is concerned the development of some of its different aspects has already been outlined in previous chapters. The four main Sunni schools of law became established in the third/ninth century and have remained to this day while some of the less popular schools gradually died out. The science of *Ḥadīth* as a distinct discipline began in the second century with a written compilation of the first collection of prophetic sayings under the Umayyad caliph, 'Umar ibn 'Abd al-'Azīz. It also became a fully established discipline in the third/ninth century when the authoritative collections were assembled. Likewise the religious and grammatical study of the text of the Holy Quran which had been cultivated informally from the beginning became a well-established discipline from he second century onward.

As for theology whose full discussion requires a separate chapter it began in the second century with the debates over freewill and determinism as well as over the nature of the Quran. The explicit Kharijite and Murji'ite discussions of the relation of faith to works in the second century must also be considered as a beginning for later theological developments. But again it was in the third century that theology in the Sunni world became fully established with the Mu'tazilites who were dominant during the early Abbasid period. As is well known, he Mu'tazilites applied the use of reason to the understanding of the tenets of revelation and arrived at a conception of the Divine Attributes and the Quran which was opposed by the religious community at large so that within a few centuries they disappeared as an influential theological school.

Meanwhile, towards the end of the third century, Abu'l-Ḥasan al-Ash'arī, who had himself been a Mu'tazilite, rebelled against heir views and founded the dominant Ash'arite school of heology. Although the domination of Ash'arism is not as complete as is usually thought, nevertheless, to the extent hat theology was cultivated in the Sunni world, the Ash'arite school became the most important force. Opposed to the rationalistic tendency of the Mu'tazilites, Ash'arite theology believed in the subservience of reason to revelation but neverheless encouraged a rational understanding of the faith. The Māturīdī school, which also developed about the same time as Ash'arism, chartered an intermediate course between the Mu'tazilites and Ash'arites and although never widespread has continued to have adherents to the present day.

In addition to these schools of theology which grew in the Sunni world and have been taught in the traditional schools or *madrasahs*, one must also remember the role of the teachings of Sufism even in this domain. Not only were some of the early Sufis like al-Muḥāsibī also theologians, but gradually, after the sixth/twelfth century, what one might call 'mystical theology' based on the teachings of the Sufi masters entered into the general field of Sunni theology. Especially after the Mongol invasion, when much of religious education was administered by Sufi organizations, this form of instruction of spiritual doctrines entered into the curriculum of many religious schools. Henceforth in the Sunni world the teachings of Sufism in its intellectual aspect were often taught combined with the more external and formal Ash'arite theology. There have been many Sufi masters until modern times who have combined the exposition of Sufi doctrine with theology especially Ash'arism.

An important aspect of Sunnism, especially as far as its comparison with Shi'ism is concerned, is political theory. All Sunnis accept the first four caliphs, Abū Bakr, 'Umar, 'Uthmān and 'Alī, as true vice-gerents (*khalīfah*) of the Prophet who fulfilled this function in its fullness so that they are called the 'rightly-guided caliphs' (*al-khulafā' al-rāshidūn*). With the establishment of the Umayyad caliphate the name of the institution of caliphate was continued, but in reality the Islamic caliphate was transformed into an Arab kingdom. That is why later Sunni jurists accepted only the first four caliphs as full embodiments of the ideal of caliphate.

The political theory of the caliphate was however elaborately developed gradually even if it was not practically realized to its fullness at the time. The Sunni political theorists when discussing the theory of the caliphate usually referred to it as the imamate by which they meant the office of the person whose duty it was to administer the *Sharī'ah* and act as judge. But since this term is particularly associated with Shi'ism it is better to refer to the Sunni institution as the caliphate and use the term imamate in connection with Shi'ism to avoid confusion.

The earlier Sunni authorites conceived of the caliphate as the legitimate political institution of the Islamic community. As there is only one community (*ummah*) and one Divine Law or *Sharī'ah*, so is there ideally one caliph who rules over the community and whose duty it is to protect the community and administer the *Sharī'ah* in conformity with the view of the *'ulamā'*. Later, when the caliphate became weakened politically and powerful kings ruled over the Muslim world, this theory was somewhat revised to include the caliph, the sultan and the Divine Law. The caliph symbolized the unity of the community and the supremacy of the Divine Law, while the sultan held actual temporal, military and political power and was supposed to enforce and uphold the Law and protect the community. In both its phases, therefore, Sunni political theory is characterized by the institution of the caliphate whose task is not to interpret the Divine Law and religious matters in general, but to administer the Law and act as judge in accordance with this Law.

It is with respect to the general background of Islam that Shi'ism must be understood. The Shi'ah are those who believe that the right of succession to the Prophet belongs solely to his family and who follow the family of the Prophet (*ahl al-bait*) as their source of inspiration and guidance for the understanding of the Quranic revelation brought by the Prophet. The members of his family are the channel through whom the teachings and the grace, or ***barakah***, of the revelation reach the Shi'ah. In a sense one can call Shi'ism the 'Islam of 'Alī', as Sunnism can also in a certain sense be called the 'Islam of Abū Bakr'.

Within this segment of the Islamic community called the Shi'ah there are further distinctions to be made depending upon the number of Imams that are accepted after the Prophet. The main body of Shi'ism, in both number and its centrality within the traditional religious spectrum, is Twelve-imam Shi'ism. Then there is Seven-imam Shi'ism or Isma'ilism and Five-imam Shi'ism or Zaidism. Twelve-imam Shi'ism is the official religion of Persia and the majority of the population belongs to this school. It also constitutes half the population of Iraq and has a substantial following in India, Pakistan, Afghanistan, Lebanon and certain lands of East Africa. Isma'ilism is more diffuse in its geographic distribution. It has sizeable following in India, Pakistan and East Africa and smaller Isma'ili communities are found in many countries such as Iran, Syria, and Egypt. As for Zaidism, it is found today in the Yemen, where the majority of the population are Zaidis. There are also small groups such as the 'Alawīs of Syria and the Druzes of Syria and Lebanon which have branched off from the main body of Shi'ism into heterodox sects. The Shi'ites constitute about a fifth of the total Muslim population, although the influence of Shi'ism on the total intellectual and spiritual life of Islam is much greater than what this quantitative relation might imply.

In this chapter we shall limit our treatment to Twelve-imam Shi'ism and Isma'ilism which are the two most important branches, twelve and seven being, like the days of the weeks and months of the year or the planets and signs of Zodiac, archetypal numbers which determine the rhythm of human existence. In order to understand their doctrine however, it is helpful first of all to gain some familiarity with their general history.

Upon the death of the Prophet a small group of men like Salmān, Abū Dharr and Miqdād sided with 'Alī, while the majority of the Meccans swore allegiance to Abū Bakr who was thus chosen as caliph. During his caliphate, as well as those of 'Umar and 'Uthmān, the Shi'ites or followers of 'Alī led a quiet life while 'Alī himself retired from public activity and devoted his time to the training and instruction of his disciples who, meanwhile, became more numerous. Then he became himself caliph and for a short period of five years the Shi'ites realized their ideal to which they always look back, although the years of 'Alī's caliphate were full of hardship.

With the establishment of the Umayyad dynasty Shi'ism entered into the most difficult period of its history during which it was openly and secretly opposed and often persecuted. Only the rule of 'Umar ibn 'Abd al-'Azīz marks an exception to this general trend. Moreover, it was during this period that the grandson of the Prophet, Ḥusain, was massacred in Kerbala marking a tragedy which has coloured the whole subsequent history of Islam and particularly Shi'ism. During the Umayyad period several Shi'ite uprisings did take place which, however, were crushed each time. Yet, this very opposition weighed heavily upon the shoulders of the Umayyads and played a major role in their downfall.

The revolt of Abū Muslim in Khurasan was based on strong Shi'ite sentiment and, in fact, he asked allegiance of the people for the 'House of the Prophet'. Yet, once the Abbasids came to power, their opposition to the Shi'ah was hardly less severe than that of the Umayyads. Only at the beginning of the third Islamic century and especially during the reign of al-Ma'mūn did Shi'ism have the opportunity to function relatively freely, in fact to the extent that the eighth Imam—'Alī al-Riḍā—was chosen as the successor of al-Ma'mūn. But after the poisoning and later the death of al-Ma'mūn the situation became difficult once again, to such a degree that the new caliph ordered the tomb of Imam Ḥusain in Kerbala to be destroyed and turned into a field.

The fourth century marks the first period in which Shi'ism

eally flourished. The Buyids, who were Shi'ites, controlled all f Persia and wielded power even in Baghdad. The Fatimids neanwhile conquered Egypt and established an Isma'ili aliphate in North Africa that rivalled the Abbasid caliphate in ower. Henceforth Shi'ism continued to flourish even after the oming of the Ayyubids and the Seljuqs, both of whom were trong supporters of Sunnism. It is true that in certain regions uch as Syria and the Lebanon, the failure of the Fatimids efore the Crusaders and the singular success of the Ayyubids, articularly Ṣalāḥ al-Dīn, before the same forces, caused hi'ism to decline in particular areas in favour of Sunnism, but n general between the fifth and ninth century Shi'ism spread radually, especially in Persia, while it declined in Egypt and North Africa. The Isma'ili movement of Alamut must also be nentioned in this connection although after the Mongol invasion t was outwardly crushed and went underground.

Meanwhile, the success of Twelve-imam Shi'ism can be auged by the conversion of the Il-Khanid king, Maḥmūd Khudābandah, to Shi'ism. Already the background was prepared for the Safavids, who in the tenth/sixteenth century, onquered all of Persia and established Twelve-imam Shi'ism s the state religion. Under them, gradually, all of that country ecame Shi'ite and continues to be so to the present day. Meanwhile Shi'ism has persisted in the Yemen which was eparated from the main current of political events in other Muslim lands. In India, also, sizeable Twelve-imam Shi'ah ommunities were established and even ruled for some time in he south. Also India eventually provided a base for Isma'ilism vhose spiritual centre finally found its home in that land.

In discussing Shi'ism it is logical to begin with the Twelve-mam school because of its centrality and the balance it preserves etween the exoteric and esoteric dimensions of the revelation. As far as the intellectual life of Twelve-imam Shi'ism is concerned it can be divided into four periods for the sake of convenience in studying it. This division has, in fact, been carried ut by Corbin in his many studies on Shi'ism. The first period s that of the Prophet and Imams stretching from the life-time f the Prophet to the major occultation (*al-ghaybat al-kubrā*) f the Twelfth Imam, or Mahdi, in the year 329/940. During his period, which is unique in the history of Shi'ism, the

Prophet and Imams lived among men whom they instructed in the meaning of the Divine Law as well as the esoteric sciences. Upon the knowledge and experience of this period rests the whole spiritual and religious life of Shi'ism. During this period the Divine Law was revealed through the Prophet and its interpretation made known by the Prophet and the Imams.

The second period may be considered as stretching from the time of occultation of the Mahdi to the Mongol invasion, not only because of the great changes brought about by this event but also because this last date corresponds to the life of Khwājah Naṣīr al-Dīn al-Ṭūsī. With this remarkable genius, who was an outstanding mathematician, astronomer and philosopher Shi'ite theology reaches its height. He may, in fact, be considered in many ways as the greatest of the Shi'ite theologians. This period is marked by the appearance of authoritative collections of *Ḥadīth* and religious doctrine which form the very substance of Shi'ite religious life. It begins with Kulainī, the author of the *Uṣūl al-kāfī* which is the most outstanding compilation of the traditions of the Shi'ite Imams. It is also the age of Ibn Bābūyah, Shaikh Mufīd and Muḥammad ibn Ḥasan al-Ṭūsī who are the authors of the main traditional sources of Shi'ite religious sciences. Also during this period Sayyid Sharīf al-Raḍī compiled the sayings of 'Alī in the *Nahj al-balāghah* which after the Quran and prophetic *Ḥadīth* is the most important work in Shi'ism.

The third period, stretching from the Mongol invasion to the establishment of the Safavids, is the most obscure because the sources of this period have not been well studied. Just as the political and social history of this period is not well known, due to the general turmoil of the age and the presence of so many local dynasties, so the details of the religious life of Shi'ism in this age are as yet unknown. It can however be said that in general during this period the school of Naṣīr al-Dīn continued both in theology and philosophy as can be seen by such figures as his students 'Allāmah Ḥillī, one of the most prolific Shi'ite authors and Quṭb al-Dīn al-Shīrāzī, the well-known philosopher and scientist. Moreover, the Sufi school of Central Asia connected mostly with the name of Najm al-Dīn Kubrā became combined with the school of Ibn 'Arabī often in the bosom of Shi'ism as can be seen in the works of such a figure as Sa'd al-Dīn Ḥamūyah.

Ibn 'Arabī, the great Sufi master from Andalusia who settled and died in Damascus, exercised an immense influence over Shi'ite gnostics at this time. His doctrine became integrated with Shi'ism in the hands of such men as Sayyid Ḥaidar Āmulī, Ibn Abī Jumhūr and Ibn Turkah. Sufi metaphysics was even influential within Shi'ite theology, not to speak of the theosophy (*al-ḥikmat al-ilāhīyah*) which was cultivated at this time in Persia under the influence of the Illuminationist (*ishrāqī*) doctrines of Suhrawardī.

The fourth period, extending from the Safavid period to the present, began with the remarkable Safavid renaissance. Shi'ite law and theology were revived leading finally to the composition of the immense religious encyclopedia, the *Biḥār al-anwār*, composed by Muḥammad Bāqir Majlisī. Shi'ite religious and metaphysical doctrines found some of their most outstanding expositors in Mīr Dāmād, Bahā' al-Dīn al-'Āmilī, one of the many Shi'ites from Jabal 'Āmil in Lebanon who had come to Persia, and Sadr al-Dīn Shīrazī, usually known as Mullā Ṣadrā. This last named, who is perhaps the greatest Islamic philosopher or more correctly theosopher (*ḥakīm*), founded a new intellectual dimension in Islam, combining the teachings of Ibn 'Arabī, Suhrawardī, Ibn Sīnā and Naṣīr al-Dīn in the texture of Shi'ism. Henceforth, Shi'ite learning flourished in Persia and Iraq and also in Lebanon and certain centres in India. The outstanding figures of the Safavid period have had many disciples and followers in the later centuries, men who have kept their religious and intellectual teachings alive to the present day.

As for the history of Isma'ilism, it is more difficult to study because of the esoteric nature of the movement itself and the lack of sources concerning its early life. The information given in standard histories is usually from the point of view of those who opposed Isma'ilism and there are few Isma'ili works on their own early history. Only the *'Uyūn al-akhbār* of the Yemeni *dā'ī*, Idrīs 'Imād al-Dīn, and a few extant works of similar nature represent the Isma'ili point of view itself. That is why Muslim and Western scholars alike have not been able to agree on many important problems of early Isma'ilism.

Of course the earliest history of Isma'ilism is the same as that of Twelve-imam Shi'ism because up to the sixth Imam, Ja'far al-Ṣādiq, there is essentially one body of Shi'ites. Upon the death of this Imam, however, the Twelvers accepted Imam Mūsā al-Kāẓim whom Imam Ja'far had himself chosen as Imam, while the Isma'ilis followed his older son, Ismā'īl, who had been chosen earlier but had died while Imam Ja'far was still alive. The followers of Ismā'īl and his son Muḥammad were the first Isma'ilis, although among themselves also there existed several different views. Henceforth Twelve-imam Shi'ism and Isma'ilism separated and their histories became distinct. It is of interest to note that although small groups followed the eighth and some of the other Imams, they were never able to gain any substantial support and died out as separate movements. Twelve-imam and Seven-imam Shi'ism continued as the major forms of Shi'ism as if their existence were already guaranteed by the archetypal nature of the numbers with which they were connected.

Scholars of Isma'ilism have distinguished at least four different groups of early Isma'ilis: the early *da'wa* (which is a special Isma'ili term for religious and missionary activity) centred around the personalities of Ismā'īl and his son Muḥammad; the *da'wa* in the Yemen and North Africa leading to the establishment of the Fatimid caliphate; the movement in Syria and Mesopotamia in the third/ninth century; and finally, the Qarāmiṭah movement in Bahrain. Of course all of these movements had certain connections in as much as they propagated some aspect of religious doctrine connected with Isma'ilism. But politically and socially they cannot in any way be identified with each other. In any case, some of these movements were gradually subdued and what emerged was the well-known form of Isma'ilism connected with the name of the Fatimids in North Africa and the famous Isma'ili *dā'īs* in Persia and other eastern lands of Islam.

As for the history of Isma'ilism, Corbin, one of the most sympathetic interpreters of Isma'ili doctrine in the West, divides it into the five periods which are mentioned here to facilitate our understanding of the development of this school.

(1) The period of the early Imams up to Ismā'īl, Muḥammad and Abu'l-Khaṭṭāb.

(2) The period from Muḥammad to 'Ubaid-Allāh al-Mahdī, the founder of the Fatimid caliphate. During this period the Isma'ili imams who were three or four in number were hidden from public eye (*mastūr*) although there was much activity in the Yemen and North Africa preparing the way for the establishment of the Fatimids. The idea of being hidden (*mastūr*) must not, however, be confused with the occultation (*ghaybah*) of the Twelfth-Imam. The first implies simply being hidden from the eye of the crowd and from public notice while the second means disappearance from the physical world.

(3) The establishment of the Fatimid caliphate until the rule of the eighth caliph, al-Mustanṣir bi'llāh. During this period Isma'ilism had its own caliphate which was a powerful state competing with the Abbasids for the allegiance of the Muslim world. This period marks also the appearance of the major doctrinal works of Isma'ilism by such outstanding figures as Abū Ḥātim al-Rāzī, Qāḍī Nu'mān, Abū Ya'qūb al-Sijistānī, Ḥamīd al-Dīn al-Kirmānī and the celebrated Persian poet and Isma'ili philosopher Nāṣir-i Khusraw.

(4) The period from the eighth caliph to the Mongol invasion, during which Isma'ilism divides into two branches. After the eighth Fatimid caliph the eastern Isma'ilis, who were connected with the movement of Ḥasan al-Ṣabbāḥ and Alamut, followed Nizār ibn al-Mustanṣir and became known as the Nizari branch, while those of Egypt and the Yemen accepted his brother al-Musta'lī bi'llāh and became known as the Musta'lis. It is of interest to note, also, that the Druze movement broke away from Isma'ilism shortly before this period and followed the seventh Fatimid caliph, al-Ḥākim bi'llāh, as a 'divine incarnation'. The Musta'li branch of Isma'ilism believed in a hidden imam like Twelve-imam Shi'ism. Its chief *dā'ī* resided in the Yemen until the tenth/sixteenth century when he emigrated to India, where the chief of the community is still to be found. The Nizari branch stayed in Persia until its head, the Aga Khan, migrated to India in the nineteenth century. The present Aga Khan is the spiritual leader and imam of this branch of Isma'ilism.

(5) The period of the Mongol invasion marked by the destruction of Isma'ili power in Persia. During this period, whose history is not well known, Isma'ilism went underground and

appeared in many places within Sufi orders. There is, in fact, a definite coming together between Isma'ilism and certain forms of Sufism at this time which, however, has not been well studied. Henceforth Isma'ilism continued as a religious phenomenon without the violent political character of its earlier days. And it is as a religious community that it continues to live in the Indo-Pakistani subcontinent, East Africa, Syria and other regions, the Nizari branch being united and directed by the Aga Khan and the Musta'li branch by the chief *dā'ī* in India.

Concerning the doctrines and beliefs of Shi'ism, it is again appropriate to begin with Twelve-imam Shi'ism, then to turn to Isma'ilism, and finally to the difference between them and also the similarities and differences between Shi'ism and Sunni Islam. The major idea which underlines the whole Twelve-imam Shi'ite perspective —and is in fact shared by Isma'ilism—is the distinction between the exoteric and the esoteric to which we have alluded previously. Every manifestation must be the manifestation of something; every appearance implies a reality which 'appears'. All objectivized reality possesses an exterior and an interior aspect, this reality including not only the world of nature but also revelation which originates from the same source as nature, namely the Divine Origin of all things.

Twelve-imam Shi'ism emphasizes above all else the exoteric (*ẓāhir*), and the esoteric (*bāṭin*), aspects of religion and in this as in many other instances, joins Sufism in its point of view. The *ẓāhir* cannot exist without the *bāṭin* for then there would be nothing to manifest it and give it objective existence. And the *bāṭin* could never become objectivized and revealed without the *ẓāhir*. In this relation there lies the secret of the necessity for the existence of the Imam. A prophet in a religion brings a law from heaven to guide the lives of men. After him the revelation ceases and men are left with a law which corresponds to the exoteric aspect of the revelation. There then must come those who can interpret the inner meaning of the law and the esoteric content of the revelation.

Specifically in Islam the door of prophecy closed with the Prophet Muḥammad—upon whom be peace. He was both the exoteric and esoteric source of the revelation but in his function as revealer of Divine legislation he represents the exoteric aspect. After him there must be those who inherited his esoteric function and whose duty it is to expound the inner meaning of the Divine Law. Just as the function of prophecy, in as much as it concerns the bringing of Divine Legislation, is called *nubuwwah*, so is the function of interpreting its inner meaning to men and preserving a link with the source of the revelation called *wilāyah* in Shi'ism. In general the word *wilāyah* in Arabic, Persian and other Islamic languages means sainthood and the saint is called *walīyallāh* 'the friend of God'. But in the specific context of Shi'ism it refers, not only to the saintly life in general, but to the very function of interpreting the esoteric dimension of the revelation.

The cycle of prophecy (*dā'irat al-nubuwwah*) terminated with the Prophet who was the 'Seal of prophecy'. Henceforth no new revelation will come in the present cycle of humanity. But with the termination of this cycle there began, as already mentioned, what one might call the 'cycle of initiation' (*dā'irat al-wilāyah*), although this translation is not fully adequate to convey the idea of *wilāyah* (or *walāyat* as used in Persian works on Shi'ism). What this second cycle implies is the beginning of a chain of authorities concerned with the esoteric interpretation of the revelation and issuing directly from the Prophet himself who is the source of both the exoteric and the esoteric dimensions. Moreover, this cycle will continue until the Day of Judgment when the historic cycle itself is brought to a close. But as long as man lives on this earth the cycle of *wilāyah* subsists, providing a direct channel to the source of the revelation itself and the means whereby man can perform the fundamental operation of *ta'wīl*, of hermeneutic interpretation, of going from the exoteric to the esoteric. This basic process of *ta'wīl*, or of journeying from the *ẓāhir* to the *bāṭin*, is made possible only through the presence of the cycle of *wilāyah*. Without it there would be no way of escaping from the prison of limited forms to the abode of the celestial essences.

The person who inaugurates the cycle of *wilāyah*, and whose duty it is in every age to fulfil the function of *wilāyah*, is the Imam, whose figure is so central in Shi'ism. That is why the first Imam, 'Alī, is in fact called *walīyallāh*. In general imam means the person who stands in the front and therefore the leader of the congregational prayers. It is in this sense that this term is usually used in everyday language in Sunnism and

Shi'ism alike, such as when one says so and so is the imam of this or that mosque. It also has an honorific sense meaning one who stands at the head of the religious community. It is in this context a title bestowed on outstanding religious scholars such as Imam al-Ghazzālī or Imam al-Shāfi'ī, etc. As already pointed out it is also used in Sunni political theory to designate the ruler of the Islamic community, the imamate being in this sense synonymous with the caliphate.

But as used specifically in Shi'ism the Imam means that person who is the real ruler of the community and especially the inheritor of the esoteric teachings of the Prophet. He is one who carries the 'Muḥammadan Light' (*al-nūr al-muḥammadī*) within himself, and who fulfils the function of *wilāyah*. As already mentioned, according to both Sufism and Shi'ism there is a prophetic light which has existed from the beginning within the being of every prophet from Adam onwards. It is the source of all prophetic knowledge and is identified with the 'Muḥammadan light' or 'Muḥammadan Reality' (*al-ḥaqīqat al-muḥammadīyah*), which is the Logos. It is this Light that continues from one cycle of prophecy to another and it is this Light that exists within the Imam, by virtue of whose presence he becomes the Imam.

The Imam who fulfils the function of *wilāyah* is the sustainer of the religious law and the guarantee of its continuation. A prophet brings a Divine Law and then himself leaves the world. There are thus times when the world is without a prophet. But the Imam is always present. The earth can never be devoid of the presence of the imam be he even hidden or unknown. (لاتخلو الارض عن حجة الله) Therefore, once the Prophet of Islam has left the world it is the Imam who, in his continuous presence, sustains and preserves the religion from one period to the next. The Imam is, in fact, the sustainer and interpreter *par excellence* of the revelation. His duty is essentially threefold: to rule over the community of Muslims as the representative of the Prophet, to interpret the religious sciences and the Law to men, especially their inner meaning, and to guide men in the spiritual life. All of these functions the Imam is able to perform because of the presence of the 'Light' within him.

As a result of the presence of this Light the Imam also possesses the quality of inerrancy (*'iṣmah*), in spiritual and religious matters. He is in his inner nature as pure as the Prophet who is the source of this Light as well as his daughter, Fāṭimah, who is the mother of the Imams through 'Alī. That is why the Prophet, Fāṭimah and the Twelve Imams, are together called 'The Fourteen Pure Ones.' The *'iṣmah* of the Prophet and Imams is the logical consequence of the presence of the 'Muḥammadan Light' within them for it is this 'Light' that is the source of all revelation and ultimately all knowledge. To be guided by this 'Light' is to be protected from error. In fact only one of the many children of each Imam becomes himself the Imam, because only one carries the 'Prophetic Light' within himself. The relation between the Imams is not only a carnal one but, most of all, a spiritual connection based on the passing of this 'Light' from one Imam to another by virtue of which each becomes *'ma'ṣūm'* or 'pure' and gains authority as the sustainer and interpreter of the Divine Law.

The Imams are also the intermediaries between man and God. To ask for their succour in life is to appeal to the channel God has placed before men so as to enable man to return to Him. They are, in this sense, the extension of the personality of the Prophet. Their tombs as well as those of their descendants, the *imāmzādah* in Persian, are visited by pilgrims and are the centres of religious life. Shi'ites from all over the world make pilgrimages to the tombs of 'Alī in Najaf, that of Ḥusain in Karbela, of the seventh and ninth imams in Kazimain, of the last imams in Samarrah, of Imam Riḍā in Meshed, of his sister Ḥaẓrat Ma'ṣūmah in Qum, of the sister of Imam Ḥusain, Sayyidah Zainab, and his daughter, Sayyidah Ruqīyah, in Damascus and to many other sites. In the popular daily life of the Shi'ah these sites fulfil the same function as those of the great saints in the Sunni world such as Mūlay Idrīs in Fez, Maqām Shaikh Muḥyī al-Dīn ibn 'Arabī in Damascus, the tomb of Mawlānā Jalāl al-Dīn Rūmī in Konya, that of Hujwīrī in Lahore, the tomb of Mu'īn al-Dīn Chishtī in Ajmer, or the shrine of Shaikh 'Abd al-Qādir al-Jīlānī in Baghdad. Of course often the two categories of sacred places merge. For example in the Shi'ite world the tombs of Sufi saints who are considered the spiritual progeny of the Imams are visited frequently and in the Sunni world the tombs of the Imams and their descendants are very often visited as tombs of great saints.

The twelve Imams of Shi'ism are as follows:

(1) 'Alī ibn Abī Ṭālib, the cousin and son-in-law of the Prophet, who is the origin of the imamate and the representative of the esoteric dimension of Islam. According to the Shi'ah he was chosen at Ghadir Khumm by the Prophet as his 'entrusted' (*waṣī*) and successor.

(2) 'Ali's elder son, Imam Ḥasan, who was caliph for a short time after him and who died in Medina after retiring from public life.

(3) His younger son, Imam Ḥusain, who took the field against Yazīd, the second Umayyad caliph, and was killed with nearly the whole of his family near Karbela. His martyrdom on the tenth of Muharram (61 A.H.) marks to this day the height of the religious calendar and his tragic death symbolizes fully the ethos of Shi'ism.

(4) Imam 'Alī entitled Zain al-'Ābidīn and al-Sajjād who was the only surviving son of Imam Ḥusain, his mother being the daughter of the last Sassanid king, Yazdigird. He is especially known for his prayers *Ṣaḥīfah sajjādīyah* which is, after the *Nahj al-balāghah* of 'Alī, the outstanding literary work of the Imams containing some of the most moving lines of religious literature in Arabic. It has even been called 'The Psalm of the Family of Muḥammad'.

(5) Imam Muḥammad al-Bāqir, the son of the fourth Imam, who resided like his father in Medina. Since, at this time, the Umayyad caliphate was faced with internal revolts the Shi'ah were left more free to pursue their religious teachings. Therefore many scholars travelled to Medina to study with the fifth Imam and numerous traditions survive from him.

(6) Imam Ja'far al-Ṣādiq, the son of Imam Muḥammad al-Bāqir, who continued the propagation of Shi'ite sciences to the extent that Shi'ite law is named after him. More traditions are recorded of him and the fifth Imam than all the others combined. Thousands flocked to his religious classes including such well-known Shi'ite figures as Hishām ibn Ḥakam and the alchemist Jābir ibn Ḥayyān. Even Abū Ḥanīfah, the founder of one of the four Sunni schools of law, as well as several other well-known Sunni scholars studied with him. It is also with Imam Ja'far that Isma'ilism separated from Twelve-imam Shi'ism, the question of the successor to the sixth Imam having been made particularly difficult by the fact that the Abbasid

caliph al-Manṣūr had decided to put to death whoever was to be chosen officially by the sixth Imam as his successor thereby hoping to put an end to the Shi'ite movement.

(7) Imam Mūsā al-Kāẓim, the son of Imam Ja'far, who faced extreme hardship due to the renewed opposition of the caliphate, this time the Abbasid, against the Shi'ites. He lived much of his life in hiding in Medina until Hārūn al-Rashīd had him imprisoned and brought to Baghdad where nearby, he died. Henceforth the Imams all lived in the vicinity of the caliph and left Medina as their permanent abode.

(8) Imam 'Alī al-Riḍā, the son of Imam Mūsā al-Kāẓim, who was called by al-Ma'mūn to Marw in Khurasan where he was chosen as the successor to the caliphate. But his immense popularity and the rapid growth of Shi'ism in that region turned the caliph against him, and he was finally removed and buried in Tus or the modern city of Meshed which is today the foremost religious city in Persia. Imam Riḍā participated in many of the scholarly gatherings of al-Ma'mūn and his debates with theologians of other religions are recorded in Shi'ite sources. He is also the origin of many Sufi orders and is even called the 'Imam of initiation'.

(9) Imam Muḥammad al-Taqī, the son of Imam Riḍā, spent his life in Medina as long as al-Ma'mūn was alive, even though al-Ma'mūn, in order to keep him in Baghdad, had given his own daughter to him in marriage. Upon al-Ma'mūn's death he returned to Baghdad where he died.

(10) Imam 'Alī al-Naqī, the son of the ninth Imam, who resided in Medina until al-Mutawakkil became caliph and invited him to come to Samarra, the seat of the caliphate. But there he was very harsh with the Imam as a result of his general extreme anti-Shi'ite policy. The Imam endured the hardship until the caliph's death but did not return to Medina afterwards. He died in Samarra where his tomb and that of his son are to be found today.

(11) Imam Ḥasan al-'Askarī, the son of Imam 'Alī al-Naqī, who lived in extreme secrecy in Samarra and was closely guarded by the agents of the caliph because it was known that the Shi'ites believed his son to be the Mahdi. He married the daughter of the Byzantine emperor, Nargis Khātūn, who had embraced Islam and sold herself into slavery in order to enter

the household of the Imam, and from this marriage the twelfth Imam was born.

(12) Imam Muḥammad al-Mahdī entitled *Ṣāḥib al-zamān*, who is the last Shi'ite Imam, went into minor occultation upon the death of his father. From 260/873 to 329/940 he had four representatives (*nā'ib*) to whom he appeared from time to time and through whom he ruled the Shi'ite community. This period is thus called the minor occultation (*al-ghaibat al-ṣughrā*). Henceforth, there began the major occultation (*al-ghaibat al-kubrā*) which still endures. During this time, according to the Shi'ah, the Mahdi is alive but invisible. He is the *axis mundi*, the invisible ruler of the Universe. Before the end of time he will appear again on earth to bring equity and justice and to fill it with peace after it has been torn by war and injustice. The Mahdi is an ever-living spiritual being who guides in the spiritual path those who ask him and whose succour all the devout ask in their daily prayers. He who is spiritually qualified is, in fact, in inner contact with the Mahdi.

The twelve Imams are like the twelve constellations of the zodiac in the spiritual firmament. At their centre stands the Prophet, the sun whose light illumines these constellations. The Imams are, for the Shi'ah, a part and continuation of the spiritual reality of the Prophet and together with him, who is their source and origin in both the metaphysical and biological sense, determine the contours of that spiritual universe in which the Shi'ah live.

As far as the political aspect of Twelve-imam Shi'ism is concerned, it is directly connected with the personality of the Imam. The perfect government is that of the Imam, one which will be realized with the coming of the Mahdi who even now is the invisible ruler of the world but does not manifest himself directly in human society. In his absence every form of government is of necessity imperfect, for the imperfection of men is reflected in their political institutions. The Shi'ites, especially of Persia since the Safavid period and even before, have considered the monarchy as the least imperfect form of government in such conditions. But there have even been some like the Indian Shi'ites, Amir Ali and Tayyibji, who supported the Sunni caliphate on a purely political level although Shi'ism does not accept the caliphate in the usual sense as the legitimate

Muslim political authority. Here a distinction must be made between the ideal political ruler which Shi'ism sees in the person of the Imam and Sunnism in the caliph and acceptance of an existing situation. In the latter case there have been Shi'ites who have paid allegiance to the caliphate and even supported it. But the structure of political theory is different in the two cases, especially as it concerns the caliphate.

The distrust of all worldly government after the disappearance of the Mahdi and the early experience of the Shi'ite community made Twelve-imam Shi'ism apathetic towards political life. This is one of the features that distinguishes it from both Sunnism and Isma'ilism. The Twelvers or Imamites remained content with being observers of the political scene rather than the originators of political movements.

It must be remembered that the Safavid movement itself, which represents the one instance of major political victory for Twelve-imam Shi'ism, did not begin as a purely Shi'ite movement in the restricted sense of the word. The Safavids were a Sufi order which became so well organized and so powerful that it was able to exercise actual political authority and finally conquer all of Persia. Of course, then the Safavids made Shi'ism the state religion, but the movement itself began from a Sufi order. Furthermore, even the engagement of Twelve-imam Shi'ism in political life, made necessary by the new situation in Safavid Persia, did not completely remove the traditional distrust of the Shi'ite *'ulamā'* towards all government. It is an attitude that persists in certain quarters to this very day.

The withdrawal of the Shi'ites from political life should not however be interpreted as their withdrawal from the life of the community. On the contrary, this very apathy towards politics intensified the religious and scholarly activity of the Shi'ah. For centuries, freed from the burden and responsibility of political life, they devoted themselves wholeheartedly to the cultivation of the religious sciences and the arts and sciences in general. Most of the early Muslim educational institutions were established by the Shi'ah as were many branches of the traditional sciences. Therefore, although politically aloof, Twelve-imam Shi'ism made an immense contribution to the life of the Islamic community in domains that were more connected with the knowledge of things rather than the ruling of men.

On the other hand, the other important branch of Shi'ism, namely Isma'ilism, was marked from the beginning by an intense interest in political life and was even a revolutionary force. In this domain it has stood opposed to the view of Twelve-imam Shi'ism, but in many other questions it shares the world view of the Twelvers. Isma'ilism also emphasizes the existence of two aspects to all things, the exoteric and the esoteric. It distinguishes between the *nabī* and *walī*, the first representing the Law and the other its esoteric meaning. But whereas Twelve-imam Shi'ism preserves a balance between the exoteric and the esoteric, Isma'ilism tends to emphasize the esoteric over the exoteric and elevate the rank of the *walī* to a degree that is not found in Twelve-imam Shi'ism. The name Batini sometimes given to the Isma'ilis is as a result of their emphasis upon the esoteric or *bāṭin*.

Of great interest is the identification of the esoteric dimension of the religion, or *bāṭin*, by Isma'ilism with theosophy (*ḥikmah*), which is also called *dīn-i ḥaqq* (the religion of the truth), in Persian. If the Persian term has been used it is because the vast majority of Isma'ili works on theosophy are in Persian. Nāṣir-i Khusraw, who is perhaps the greatest Isma'ili philosopher, wrote every one of his works in Persian. In fact, Isma'ili philosophy is one of the few branches of Islamic philosophy in which the Persian texts are even more numerous than the Arabic.

Isma'ilism believes that this philosophy, or theosophy, contained in the *bāṭin* of religion leads to spiritual rebirth (*wilādat-i rūḥānī*) through which man is transformed and 'saved'. What they mean by philosophy is therefore quite different from the subject known by that name today. Much of modern philosophy is in fact not at all a 'love of wisdom' but a hatred of it so that it should appropriately be called 'misosophy'. By philosophy the Isma'ilis meant a *sophia* which was not just a mental play but a doctrine of a metaphysical and cosmological order closely connected with means of its realization.

It is not accidental that whenever Isma'ilism was strong a sudden burst of activity in the arts and sciences, and specially the intellectual sciences, took place. This connection can moreover be seen with respect to Shi'ism in general. The al-Azhar University which today is the most famous seat of learning in the Sunni world was founded by the Fatimids. The intense activity in the 'intellectual sciences' (*al-'ulūm al-'aqlīyah*) in Fatimid Egypt, shown by the presence of so many outstanding men of science such as Ibn al-Haitham and Ibn Yūnus, is directly connected with the religious structure of Isma'ilism itself. It is connected with the concept of *ḥikmah* in Isma'ilism and its direct relation with revelation.

Isma'ilism contains an elaborate metaphysics, cosmology and spiritual anthropology. In metaphysics it emphasizes Unity (*tawḥīd*) keeping a mid-way position between *ta'ṭīl* and *tashbīh*; that is, between considering the Divine as an abstract unity by refusing man the ability of understanding the meaning of His Qualities and Attributes, or by describing the Divine anthropomorphically, by comparing His Qualities and Attributes to human ones. In this fundamental point therefore it joins the view of the rest of Islamic orthodoxy.

According to Isma'ili doctrine the Origin of all things is not Pure Being but the Reality that transcends even Being and is called *Mubdi'*, He through Whose Original Act the chain of being is created. Islamic philosophy in general begins with being and is concerned with the nature of God or the Origin of the Universe as Pure Being. In Sufi metaphysics, however, the Divine Essence (*al-dhāt*) is Absolute and Infinite above all determinations, even that of Being, which is its first self-determination and the Principle of creation. Isma'ili doctrine thus joins Sufi metaphysics and Oriental metaphysics in general by considering the Supreme Principle to be at once Being and above Being. Its primordial act brings into being the order of universal existence.

The first being in the created order is the First Intellect, or Universal Intellect, which is identified with the Divine Word. It is a reality that at once veils and reveals the Supreme Name, Allah. From this highest spiritual reality, which has its own limit (*ḥadd*), there comes into being the Second Intellect and from the Second Intellect the Third Intellect which, in Isma'ilism, is identified with the Spiritual Adam (*Ādam-i rūḥānī*). This Intellect is the angelic prototype of humanity. It is the celestial Imam who is the archetype of the terrestrial Adam and of all men. The life and drama of man on earth is but a reflection of his celestial reality.

The Third Intellect, or Spiritual Adam, sought to reach the Supreme Principle without observing the proper hierarchy of the archangelic worlds above him. He committed an act of idolatory, from the metaphysical point of view, as a result of which he fell into a state of forgetfulness and stupor. Once he came to himself he realized that he had been punished by God and removed to the rank of the Tenth Intellect. He had been removed from his original abode by 'Seven spiritual worlds' which came as a result of his forgetfulness. These seven worlds are the prototypes of this world. That is why everything is governed by the cycle of seven. This world was created in order to enable man to regain his lost state, to be delivered from his own 'shadows'. And being based on its celestial model it consists of seven heavens, seven earths, seven cycles of prophecy and seven imams.

Time in which man is situated is itself 'retarded eternity', an image of the retardation caused by man's fall from the Third to the Tenth Intellect. In this spiritual anthropology time itself has a trans-historic significance being based on the forgetfulness of man which is the cause of his having fallen into the domain of time, decay and death. Separation from God comes from man's forgetfulness, a point of view that is central to Islam in general and emphasized in Sufism.

Isma'ilism has a cyclic conception of history closely allied to its metaphysical conception of time. Although a cyclic conception of time is implied in certain Twelve-imam Shi'ite sources —cyclic not in the sense of ever recurring sets of events but of other historic cycles than the present one—it is nowhere as much emphasized as in Isma'ilism. The Isma'ili works speak of a large cycle of aeons sometimes mentioned as of 360,000 years within which there are seven cycles of prophecy. Each cycle is commenced by a prophet (*nabī*) who has his esoteric representative or imam who dominates over that cycle, the seventh bringing the cycle to an end. The prophets and their imams for the present cycle of humanity are mentioned usually as:

Adam	Seth
Noah	Shem
Abraham	Ishmael
Moses	Aaron

Jesus	Simon
Muḥammad	'Alī

The seventh is the Mahdi or 'Imam of Resurrection', who does not bring a new *Sharī'ah* but reveals the inner meaning of all revelations and prepares the coming of the new cycle. Moreover, the historical cycles alter between that of epiphany and occultation, between a period when the truth is revealed and one in which it is hidden, this alteration continuing until the end of the great cycle. At this moment comes the 'Great Resurrection' (*qiyāmat al-qiyāmah*) upon which man and his celestial prototype are re-instated in their original condition. Thus through the prophets and imams the purpose of creation is fulfilled and man regains the state that he lost through his own negligence.

If one wishes to compare Twelve-imam Shi'ism and Isma'ilism it can be said that they share together, besides the general tenets of Islam, the basis concept of the imam; the esoteric and exoteric dimensions of religion and *ta'wīl* that is based on them. The first six Imams are of course also common between them with all that such a common ground implies. As far as the differences between them are considered there is first of all the fact that one accepts twelve Imams and the other seven. For example, a figure like the eighth Imam, 'Alī al-Riḍā, who plays such a major role in the life of the Shi'ah does not exist in the same capacity in the Isma'ili scheme. Also for the Twelvers the twelfth Imam, the Mahdi, is in occultation although alive, while the imam of Isma'ilism, at least the Nizari branch, is always living and present on earth among men. The idea of awaiting the appearance of the Imam (*intiẓār*) which is so important to the religious psychology of Twelve-imam Shi'ism therefore does not exist in the same sense in Isma'ilism.

The political nature of Isma'ilism and the apolitical nature of Twelve-imam Shi'ism is another distinguishing feature of these two groups as already pointed out. It appears as a paradox of history that Isma'ilism, which played such an important role in the social and political movements during the early centuries of Islamic history, should become today free of direct political association while Twelve-imam Shi'ism, which had remained aloof from political life, should be thrown in the middle of the political arena with the establishment of the Safavid dynasty. Therefore, as far as their historical careers are concerned both Twelve-imam Shi'ism and Isma'ilism have experienced direct engagement in political life. But the theological role of political action in the two communities does remain different in as much as in one the Imam is absent and in the other living among men.

Finally another distinguishing feature is the role of exotericism and esotericism. Twelve-imam Shi'ism goes to great length to emphasize the necessity of preserving a balance between the two. Even the role of the Imam is considered in both its exoteric and esoteric aspect. Isma'ilism however, especially that of Alamut, tended to emphasize the *bāṭin* or esoteric dimension above all else. Of course in the daily life of the community the exoteric elements persist for no general community of men can be simply esotericists. But the accent is somewhat different although the basic concept of the imamate exists in these two major branches of Shi'ism which are united in their belief in the imam and particular reverence for the family of the Prophet.

Concerning the differences and similarities between Shi'ism and Sunnism it can be said that, first of all, there is the difference of view concerning political rule, from the question of the political successor of the Prophet to the later institution of the general attitude of the Shi'ah towards the powers of the world and especially concerning the attitude of the '*ulamā*' towards established political authority. The Sunni '*ulamā*' have throughout history tended to support the existing political institutions in fear of creating civil strife while the Shi'ite '*ulamā*', basing their views on the role of the Imamate and the ideal rule of the Imam, have distrusted all political institutions and kept away from political authorities.

There is also a distinction between the question of intermediaries between man and God. The modern puritanical movements in the Islamic world which emphasize only the transcendence of God and discourage all intermediaries between man and God present a view that is opposed to the religious psychology of Shi'ism. But in traditional Sunnism there are intermediaries in daily religious life, the role of the intermediary being fulfilled by the Prophet and also by the saints. In Shi'ism the Prophet and the Imams together fulfil this function. In fact, in so many ways, what the traditional Sunni, especially he who is touched by the spirit of Sufism, sees in the person of the Prophet the Shi'ite sees in the Prophet and Imams together. This is demonstrated by the fact that the litanies and chants in the name of the Prophet common in the Sunni world corresponds, even in content, to those that the Shi'ah perform for the Prophet and Imams together. Nevertheless on the theological level there is some difference concerning the role of the intermediary between man and God, not that of course man prays to anyone other than to God in Shi'ite Islam any more than he does in Sunnism.

In Islam man stands before God as his vice-gerent on earth. It is, however, in seeking to approach him that he needs the spiritial intermediaries who are the Prophet, Imams and the saints. For his daily religious life the Shi'ite believer has no more need of human intermediaries between him and God than does the Sunni. Every Muslim is himself a priest, be he Sunni or Shi'ah. The presence of 'intermediaries' in Shi'ism or Sunnism is a matter concerning the inner religious life and does not in any way alter the structure of Islam as a religion without a specific priesthood or religious hierarchy which would act as intermediaries between man and God in religious rites and acts of worship.

In the field of law the difference between Sunnism and Shi'ism lies in the question of *ijtihād*. Since in Shi'ism the Imam is alive, the possibility of applying the Divine Law to new situations is always present. In fact the *mujtahid* (he who can exercise his opinion) who is in inner contact with the Imam must in each generation apply the Law to the new conditions which that generation faces. This does not, of course, mean to change the Law for the sake of circumstances but to extend it to cover any new situations that might arise. And it is the duty of each Shi'ite to follow the rulings of a living *mujtahid*. In Sunni Islam, since the third century, the gates of *ijtihād* have been closed although here again the opinions or *fatwās* of the *'ulamā'* over the ages have to a certain extent provided a continuous commentary upon the *Sharī'ah*.

In the official theological formulations of Sunnism and Shi'ism there is some difference in approach and content. Sunni theology may be characterized as more concerned with 'rational' aspects of the faith and Shi'ite theology with the 'mystical', in the sense that Sunni theology does not concern itself as much with esoteric questions as does Shi'ite theology. But here again Sufi doctrine, which is often combined with theology in the Sunni world, does provide an esoteric dimension even in the exoteric domain. Also, Shi'ite theology is more sympathetic to the arts and sciences and the 'intellectual sciences' (*al-'ulūm al-'aqlīyah*) than is Ash'arite theology. This difference is seen in the ups and downs of the career of these sciences over the centuries which have depended on the political domination of one group or another.

Finally, as far as differences between Sunnism and Shi'ism are concerned, it can be said that in one the ***barakah*** or grace of the Prophet is felt and realized through all the companions of the Prophet including his family, while in Shi'ism it is felt primarily in the family of the Prophet (*ahl al-bait*). What the companions (*ṣaḥābah*), and the family (*āl*), mean for the Sunni, the family (*āl*) in themselves means to the Shi'ah. This is even seen in the two forms of benediction upon the Prophet prevalent among the two groups. It is not that the family of the Prophet do not hold a special place in Sunnism or that the companions are unimportant in Shi'ism. But in one case one sees Islam through the whole community that surrounded the founder, and in the other through a particular elite which is his family and those who were spiritually related to him like Salmān al-Fārsī about whom the Prophet said: 'Salmān is a member of my household.' Here again it is a matter of emphasis and difference of interpretation of a single reality rather than total opposition.

As against these differences there are numerous points of similarity between Sunnism and Shi'ism which far outweigh the differences and only prove that they are two branches of the same tree. Sunni and Shi'ite Islam are united in the Quran and the Prophet, the foundation of all of Islam. They share in the principles of religion, namely in the basic doctrines of ***tawḥīd*** (unity), ***nubuwwah*** (prophecy) and eschatology (***ma'ād***). They also agree to the fact that God must be just although one emphasizes the aspect of freedom and the other necessity. One believes that whatever God does it is that which is just, while the other emphasizes that God could not be unjust. The agreement of Sunnism and Shi'ism on the principles of religion is what places them within the total orthodoxy of Islam and guarantees the presence of the basic principles of the doctrine in the formulation of both groups.

On the level of religious practice also Sunnism and Shi'ism are nearly the same. The day-to-day practice of the *Sharī'ah* is the same in both worlds. Except for one or two points, such as the amount of inheritance of the female side or temporary marriages, the rulings of the *Sharī'ah* are common to them. And in practice, the prayers, ablutions, fasting, the pilgrimage, etc. are the same save for minor differences which in the prayers are no more than the differences between the four Sunni schools of law. Only the Shi'ites add two further phrases to the call to prayers, one affirming the *wilāyah* of 'Alī and the other the importance of good works. Also, because the Imam is absent, the Shi'ites do not emphasize the Friday prayers to the same degree as the Sunnis and it lacks especially the political significance that it possesses in the Sunni world. The similarities of daily practices based on the *Sharī'ah*, from the prohibition of alcohol and pork to ways of sacrificing an animal, are so many that they cannot be enumerated here.

The similarity between Sunnism and Shi'ism in daily practice is far greater than a comparison of theological texts might show. If Shi'ism is the 'Islam of 'Alī', the *barakah* of 'Alī is also spread in the Sunni world through the presence of the Sufi orders of which he is the 'imam' even for Sunnis, and the social ramifications of these orders in guilds, orders of chivalry, etc. If one compares the daily life of a traditional Sunni, which is based on the *Sharī'ah* and punctuated with visits to the tombs of saints, reading of prayers and litanies usually written by Sufi masters like 'Abd al-Qādir al-Jīlānī and Abu'l-Ḥasan al-Shādhilī, with the daily life of the Shi'ites, one is struck by the profound resemblances. The function of the Imams and their descendants in the Shi'ite world is fulfilled in the Sunni world by the saints, who are in fact in a metaphysical sense the spiritual progeny of the Prophet and the Imams. The names of many of the Imams appear in the chain of transmission (*silsilah*) of every Sufi order. This essential identity can be 'existentially' experienced in the presence of the *barakah* of the tombs of Sufi saints on the one hand and of the Imams and their descendants on the other, although of course the particular perfume of each can be recognized.

In conclusion it can be said that Sunnism and Shi'ism are two orthodox dimensions of Islam providentially placed in this tradition to enable collectivities of different psychological and spiritual temperament to become integrated within the Islamic community. Being each an affirmation of the doctrine of unity they do not in themselves destroy the profound unity of Islam whatever their formal differences may be. They are rather two ways of asserting the truth of the *Shahādah, Lā ilāha ill'Allāh.* They are two streams which originate from the same fountain, which is their unique source, namely, the Quranic revelation. And they finally pour into one sea which is the Divine Unity whose means of realization each contains within itself. To have lived either of them fully is to have lived as a Muslim and to have realized that Truth for the sake of whose revelation the Quran was made known to men through the Prophet of Islam.

wa'llāhu a'lam.

Suggestions for further reading

Chapman, J. A. (trans.), *Maxims of Ali*, Lahore, Muhammad Ashraf. An English translation of some of the sayings of Ali whose totality is found in the *Nahj al-balāghah.*

Corbin, H., *En Islam iranien*, 4 vols., Paris Gallimard, 1971-72. A monumental work summarizing a life-time of research on Islam in Persia. The first volume contains a detailed study of Shi'ism in its esoteric and metaphysical aspects while the third volume is devoted to Sufism in its various manifestations in Persia.

—*Histoire de la philosophie islamique*, Part II. A penetrating description of both Twelve-imam Shi'ism and Isma'ilism concentrating especially on the exposition of their metaphysical doctrines with some attention given to their religious history.

—*L'Imâm caché et la rénovation de l'homme en théologie shi'ite, Eranos Jahrbuch*, (Zurich), XXVIII, 1959. Contains a profound study of the figure of the Twelfth Imam and his role in the spiritual life in Shi'ism.

—*Pour une morphologie de la spiritualité shi'ite, Eranos Jahrbuch*, XXIX, 1960. A general study of the structure of Shi'ite spiritually carried out with much sympathy for the Shi'ite perspective.

—*Le Combat spirituel du shi'isme, Eranos Jahrbuch*, XXX, 1961. The role of the Imam in the inner spiritual life of Shi'ism.

—*Au "pays" de l'Imâm caché, Eranos Jahrbuch* XXXII, 1963. A description of the 'intermediate' spiritual world or the 'eighth climate' which is the abode of the Hidden Imam and the meaning of this world for the spiritual life.

Corbin, H., *Le Temps cyclique dans le mazdéisme et dans l'ismaélisme, Eranos Jahrbuch*, XXI, 1951. The concept of cyclic time in Isma'ilism analyzed and compared with Mazdaean ideas on time.

—(ed. and trans.) *Trilogie ismaélienne*, Tehran, Institut Franco-Iranien, 1961. The text and French translation of three works of different periods connected with Isma'ilism as well as Shi'ism and Sufism with a comparative study by Corbin of these three aspects of Islam.

al-Ḥillī, 'Allāmah Hasan b. Yūsuf, (trans. W. M. Miller) *Al-bābu'l-hādī 'ashar; a Treatise on the Principles of Shi'ite Theology*, London, Royal Asiatic Society, 1928. The translation of one of the most popular summaries of Twelve-imam Shi'ite theology which has served as a standard text in religious schools for centuries.

Hollister, J. N., *The Shi'a of India*, London, Luzac, 1953. A historical survey of Shi'ism in India containing also a general study of Shi'ite doctrines and beliefs.

Ibn Bābawaih, trans. A. A. Fyzee, *A Shi'ite Creed*, London, Oxford University Press, 1952. A literal translation of an authoritative traditional statement of Shi'ite beliefs.

Ivanow, W., *Ismaili Literature, A Bibliographical Survey*, Tehran, University Press, 1963. A thorough survey of Isma'ili works compiled by one of the leading expositors of Isma'ili doctrine and history.

—*Studies in Early Persian Ismailism*, Leiden, Brill, 1948. A historical outline of the early phases of the Isma'ili movement in Persia.

—(ed. and trans.), *Kalāmi Pīr, a Treatise on Ismaili Doctrine*, Bombay, Ismaili Society, 1955. An English translation of a standard statement of Isma'ili beliefs of the later period after the Alamut reform.

Massignon, L., *Salmān Pāk et les prémises spirituelles de l'Islam iranien*, Paris, Société des Etudes Iraniennes, 1934. A monograph on the significance of Salmān for Shi'ite Islam containing profound observations on the role of this figure in the religious consciousness of the Persians.

—*Die Ursprünge und die Bedeutung des Gnostizismus in Islam, Eranos-Jahrbuch*, 1937. Gnostic doctrines of Isma'ilism considered in their origin and significance.

Nāsir-i Khusraw, *Le 'Livre réunissant les deux sagesses' ou harmonie de la philosophie grecque et de la theosophie ismaélienne*, ed. and trans. H. Corbin and M. Mo'īn, Tehran, Institut Franco-Iranien, 1953. The Persian text with French translation of the outstanding philosophical work of Nāṣir-i Khusraw containing a long introduction by Corbin on Isma'ili philosophy.

Nasr, S. H., *An Introduction to Islamic Cosmological Doctrines*, Cambridge, Harvard University Press, 1964. An analysis of the cosmological aspect of the *Epistles* of the Ikhwān al-Safā' which is associated with the Shi'ite point of view and a discussion of the relation of Shi'ism to the arts and sciences in Islam.

Salmin, Muhammad Ali al-Haj, *Ali the Caliph*, Bangalore, Modi Power Printing Works, 1931. An account of the life and teachings of Ali from the traditional point of view and the translation of some of his sayings and sermons.

Strothmann, R., *Die Zwölfer Schi'a. Zwei religionsgeschichte Charakterbilder aus der Mongolenzeit*, Leipzig, Harrassowitz, 1926. A noteworthy study of two leading Shi'ite theologians through whom the general religious structure of Shi'ism is described.

—*Gnosis-Texte der Ismailiten*, Göttingen, Akademie der Wissenschaft, 1943. A translation with commentary of some important Isma'ili metaphysical texts.

al-Ṭūsī, Naṣīr, al-Dīn, ed. and trans. W. Ivanow, *Rawḍat al-taslīm* or *Taṣawwurāt*, Leiden, Brill, 1950. An English translation of a summary of Isma'ili beliefs after the Alamut reform by the outstanding Twelve-imam Shi'ite theologian, al-Tūsī, when he was in the bondage of Isma'ili rulers in Khurasan.

Additional suggestions from Chapter II (p. 66)

Cragg, K., *The Event of the Qur'an*, London, Allen & Unwin, 1971. A sympathetic attempt to understand the meaning of the Quranic revelation as an event which transformed the world about it.

—*The Mind of the Qur'an*, London, Allen & Unwin, 1973. The sequel to *The Event of the Qur'an* in which the reception of the Quranic revelation by the early Islamic community is discussed.

Izutsu, T., *God and Man in the Koran*, Tokyo, the Keio Institute of Cultural and Linguistic Studies, 1964. Contains a scholarly and penetrating study of the language of the Quran, especially as it pertains to the relationship between man and God.

Glossary of technical terms

adhān, the call to prayer announced from the top of minarets and other places to draw the attention of the community to the time for the canonical prayers.

ahl al-kitāb, literally 'people of the book', the Quranic expression used to describe people to whom a holy book has been revealed. At the beginning of Islamic history the term was used in reference to the Christians, Jews and the Sabeans and later with the conquest of Persia to the Zoroastrians. But the principle was applied afresh whenever Muslims encountered a genuine living tradition so that later Hindus and Buddhists were also described by certain Islamic spiritual authorities as 'people of the book'.

al-'ālim (pl. *'ulamā'*), literally 'he who knows', but more specifically the scholar versed in the religious sciences and therefore authorized to interpret these sciences and especially the Divine Law.

'aql, both intellect, in its original sense as *nous*, and reason (*ratio*), depending on the context in which it is used and the way it is qualified.

barakah, grace, the spiritual presence and influence which is at once 'supernatural' and flowing within the arteries of the cosmos.

bāṭin, the inward aspect of revelation and of manifestation both cosmic and supracosmic; and also a name of God, who is described in the Quran as being both the Inward (*al-bāṭin*) and the Outward (*al-ẓāhir*).

dhikr, meaning literally to mention, to invoke and to remember, it is the central technique for spiritual realization in Sufism.

fiṭrah, the original nature of man and of things.

ghaflah, negligence or forgetfulness of God, which in Sufism is considered as the major impediment to spiritual realization and in Islam more generally speaking as the root of most sins.

ḥadīth (pl. *aḥādīth*), literally saying or tradition but more specifically in the context of religion the sayings of the Prophet of Islam, which are one of the major pillars of Islam, both as a religion and as a civilization and culture. In Shi'ism the sayings of the Imams are also incorporated in the collection of *Ḥadīth*, although still distinguished from the sayings of the Prophet.

ḥadīth qudsī, 'sacred tradition', a small number of *hadīth* in which God speaks in the first person through the Prophet. This collection is of particular importance for Islamic esotericism.

ḥajj, the pilgrimage to Mecca which is incumbent on all Muslims who have the means at least once in their life-time.

ḥaqīqah, at once the 'Truth', the spiritual essence of things, and ultimate reality. Contrasted in the context of Sufism with *Sharī'ah* and *ṭarīqah*.

ḥikmah, wisdom, *sapientia*; also the school of 'theosophy', which in certain contexts is used synonymously with traditional Islamic philosophy.

'ibādah (pl. *'ibādāt*), worship under all its forms. In Islamic law all injunctions are divided into those which deal with various forms of worship (*'ibādāt*) and those which deal with human relations and transactions (*mu'āmalāt*).

ijmā', the consensus of opinion of the community, or more particularly the classes of learned men (*'ulamā'*), concerning various religious problems.

ijtihād, the exercising of authority and giving of independent judgment concerning matters pertaining to the religious sciences and more specifically to Islamic law on the part of those who possess the necessary traditional qualifications.

imām, literally he who stands at the front, hence the leader of the daily prayers and also he who is the leader of the community. In the Sunni world the term is also used as an honorific title for outstanding religious scholars while in Shi'ism 'Imam' refers to the person who carries within himself the special initiatic power issuing from the prophetic revelation.

īmān, religious faith and also the more inward dimension of religion which possesses the quality of intense faith and fervor.

al-insān al-kāmil, the universal or perfect man who contains within himself all the possibilities of universal existence and who finds his embodiment in the prophets and saints, foremost among them for Muslims being of course the Prophet of Islam, who is *al-insān al-kāmil par excellence* in Islamic esotericism.

'irfān, gnosis or divine knowledge.

jihād, holy war, of which the 'lesser' is against external obstacles to the establishment and functioning of the divine order and the 'greater' against the inward forces which prevent man from realizing God within the centre of his being.

khalīfah, vice-gerent or lieutenant; in the political domain, it refers to the representatives of the Prophet in his politico-social and juridical functions who came to be known as caliphs and in the spiritual sense it is a designation for the universal man in his function as God's vice-gerent before the whole of creation.

mahdī, literally the 'guided one', but in the context of Islamic history the title of the person who will be sent to re-establish justice on earth before the end of time and to prepare the second advent of Christ. In Sunnism the identity of the *mahdī* is not specified while in Shi'ism he is identified with the Twelfth Imam.

ma'rifah, divine knowledge or gnosis, which follows the love (*maḥabbah*) and the fear (*makhāfah*) of God.

mu'āmalah (pl. *mu'āmalāt*), the portion of Islamic law dealing with transactions (see *'ibādah*).

mujtahid, he who because of his mastery of the religious sciences and integrity of character has gained the right to practise *ijtihād*, that is, give independent judgment on religious problems.

nabī, prophet, he who brings tidings from the invisible world.

nafs, the soul or the psyche which stands between the body (*jism*) and the spirit or intellect (*rūḥ* or *'aql*).

qiyās, in logic, syllogism, and in the religious sciences, analogical thinking; in certain schools of jurisprudence it is one of the bases of the *Sharī'ah*.

rasūl, a particular class of prophets who bring a message for a particular humanity.

Shahādah, the testimony of faith in Islam consisting of the two formulas *Lā ilāha illa'llāh*, 'There is no divinity but the Divine' and *Muḥammadun rasūl Allāh*, 'Muhammad is the messenger of God'.

Sharī'ah, the Divine Law of Islam and more generally the religious law of any revealed religion.

shirk, the cardinal and only unforgivable sin in Islam, which consists of envisaging a partner for the Divinity and therefore of compromising God's inviolable Unity.

sunnah, the way of living and acting of the Prophet of Islam, which has become the traditional ideal according to which Muslims seek to mold their own lives.

tafsīr, commentary upon the Quran, which is usually distinguished from *ta'wīl*, the hermeneutic and esoteric interpretation of the Holy Book.

tajallī, the theophany of God's Names and Qualities, which in Islamic metaphysics is expressed in the symbolism of the reflection of an object in a mirror or shiny surface so as to emphasize that the 'object' is reflected without entering into the mirror. The Truth is reflected in this world through *tajallī* and therefore does not enter into the world, nor is it affected by the becoming inherent in this herent to this world.

ṭarīqah (pl. *ṭuruq*), literally the path or the way, hence the spiritual path leading to God. The Sufi order, which embodies the discipline necessary for spiritual realization, is thus called the *ṭarīqah*, the path to God.

taṣawwuf, the inner or esoteric dimension of Islam, which acquired this name from the 2nd/8th century onward, a name which is the source for the word Sufism.

tawḥīd, Unity, at once of the Divine and of all things and also the integration which leads to the awareness and realization of Unity.
ta'wīl, literally 'to take something back to its origin', hence the esoteric and spiritual interpretation of both the Quran and creation, the esoteric or the inward being also the origin and the beginning.
ummah, the Islamic community, as defined by the adherence of its members to the Islamic revelation and the traditions of the Prophet of Islam. By extension other religious communities are also known to Muslims as the ***ummah*** of different prophets.
waḥdat al-wujūd, the transcendent unity of being, the central and characteristic doctrine of *Sufi* metaphysics, formulated explicitly for the first time by Muhyī al-Dīn ibn 'Arabī.
waḥy, revelation in its technical Islamic sense, which is distinguished clearly from inspiration (*ilhām*), the first being reserved exclusively for prophets and the second being available in principle to all men.
ẓāhir, the outward or the external aspect of manifestation and also of God, ***al-Ẓāhir*** being a Divine Name, contrasted with ***al-bāṭin***, the inward.

Index